D0546810

Uzbekistan Travel Guide 2024(Updated)

Uncover Uzbekistan's Hidden Gems: A Traveler's Handbook for Finding and Enjoying the Less Touristy Areas of a Diverse and Beautiful Country

William J.Phillips

Copyright 2023, WILLIAM J. PHILLIPS. All rights reserved. No part of this book may be reproduced, distributed, or transmitted in any form or by any means, including photocopying, recording, or other electronic or mechanical methods, without the prior written permission of the copyright owner, except in the case of brief quotations embodied in critical reviews and certain other noncommercial uses permitted by copyright law.

TABLE OF CONTENTS

Chapter 1 Introduction to Uzbekistan

Uzbekistan, nestled within the heart of Central Asia, is a landlocked country primarily situated between the Syr Darya and Amu Darya rivers. With a population of approximately 34.8 million people, it covers an expanse of 447,400 square kilometers, making it slightly larger than California or four times the size of Virginia. The capital and largest city, Tashkent, boasts a history spanning over 2,000 years and has evolved into a modern metropolis that beautifully blends ancient and contemporary architectural marvels.

Having gained independence from the Soviet Union in 1991, Uzbekistan functions as a presidential republic with a bicameral parliament. Shavkat Mirziyoyev, the incumbent president, was reelected in 2021, securing an impressive 80% of the vote. The official languages of the nation are Uzbek and Russian, with Tajik widely spoken in certain regions. The predominant religion is Islam, predominantly Sunni, alongside a Christian, mostly Orthodox, minority. The Uzbek som (UZS) serves as the official currency, with an exchange rate of approximately 10,500 UZS per US dollar as of October 2021.

Uzbekistan boasts a rich and diverse cultural heritage, influenced by the tapestry of civilizations and peoples that have inhabited or traversed its lands throughout history. The nation is home to some of the world's oldest and most renowned cities, including Samarkand, Bukhara, Khiva, and Shakhrisabz, all of which were once integral parts of the legendary Silk Road connecting China and Europe. These cities, designated UNESCO World Heritage Sites, stand as living testimonials to the remarkable architecture, art, and craftsmanship of the Islamic world during the Timurid era. In addition to its historical marvels, Uzbekistan also shines through its vibrant and colorful folk culture, expressed through music, dance, literature, cuisine, and handicrafts.

Beyond its cultural treasures, Uzbekistan dazzles with its striking and varied natural beauty. The country's landscapes range from deserts and mountains to valleys and lakes. It is home to several national parks and reserves dedicated to safeguarding its flora and fauna. Among them are the Ugam-Chatkal National Park, featuring snow-capped peaks, alpine meadows, and lush forests; the Nuratau-Kyzylkum Biosphere Reserve, inhabited by rare wildlife such as the Persian leopard, Bukhara deer, an Severtsov's sheep; and the Aral Sea Biosphere Reserve, aimed at restoring the ecosystem of the shrinking Aral Sea. Uzbekistan further offers a plethora of opportunities for outdoor enthusiasts and adventure seekers, with activities ranging from hiking and skiing to rafting, horseback riding, and camel treks.

Uzbekistan stands as a nation that caters to the interests of anyone seeking to explore its rich history, diverse culture, and natural wonders. It beckons visitors with open arms, extending its renowned hospitality and warmth. Uzbekistan is a land that astonishes and captivates with its diversity and allure, making it a destination that should undoubtedly find a place on every traveler's bucket list.

Geographical Overview

Uzbekistan has a continental climate, with hot and dry summers and cold and snowy winters. The average annual temperature ranges from 10°C in the north to 16°C in the south.

Uzbekistan has a diverse terrain, consisting of plains, deserts, mountains, and rivers. The largest and most dominant feature of Uzbekistan is the Kyzylkum Desert, which covers about 60% of the country's territory and is one of the largest deserts in the world. The Kyzylkum Desert is mostly sandy and gravelly, with sparse vegetation and wildlife. The desert is also rich in natural resources, such as gold, uranium, copper, and natural gas.

Another major feature of Uzbekistan is the Aral Sea, which was once the fourth largest lake in the world, but has shrunk dramatically since the 1960s due to irrigation projects that diverted water from its main sources, the Amu Darya and Syr Darya rivers. The Aral Sea is now divided into several smaller lakes, some of which are saline and toxic, while others are freshwater and support fishing and tourism. The Aral Sea disaster has caused severe environmental and social problems for the region, such as desertification, salinization, pollution, health issues, and economic decline.

Uzbekistan also has some mountainous regions, mainly in the east and south. The Pamir Mountains are part of the Himalayan range and extend into Uzbekistan's southeastern corner. They are the highest mountains in Central Asia and include some of the world's highest peaks, such as Ismoil Somoni Peak (7,495 meters) and Lenin Peak (7,134 meters). The Pamir Mountains are known for their glaciers, alpine lakes, and diverse flora and fauna. They are also home to some ethnic minorities, such as the Pamiris and the Wakhi.

The Fergana Valley is a fertile and densely populated region that spans across Uzbekistan, Kyrgyzstan, and Tajikistan. It is surrounded by the Tien Shan Mountains in the north and the Pamir-Alai Mountains in the south. The Fergana Valley is one of the oldest and most important cultural centers of Central Asia, with a history dating back to ancient times. It is also one of the most ethnically diverse and politically sensitive areas of Uzbekistan, as it hosts various ethnic groups, such as Uzbeks, Tajiks, Kyrgyzs, Uyghurs, Russians, and others.

A Glimpse into Hidden Gems

Uzbekistan has many hidden gems that are not as well-known or visited by tourists, but offer a unique and authentic experience of the country. Here are some of them:

The Savitsky Museum in Nukus: This museum is one of the most remarkable and unexpected collections of art in the world. It was founded by Igor Savitsky, a Russian painter and collector who rescued thousands of avant-garde and folk artworks from Soviet censorship and repression. The museum displays over 90,000 pieces of art, ranging from ancient Zoroastrian artifacts to modern abstract paintings. The museum is also known as the Louvre of the Steppes, as it showcases the rich and diverse cultural heritage of Central Asia.

The Surkhandarya region in Termez: This region is located in the southernmost part of Uzbekistan, bordering Afghanistan. It is one of the oldest and most historically significant areas of Central Asia, as it was the birthplace of Buddhism, Zoroastrianism, and Islam in the region. It is also the site of many ancient civilizations, such as Bacteria, Kushan, and Sogdia. The region has many archaeological and architectural wonders, such as the Buddhist stupa of Fayaz Tepe, the Zoroastrian fire temple of Jarkurgan, and the Islamic mausoleum of Al-Hakim al-Termizi.

The Nuratau Mountains in Nurata: This mountain range is located in the eastern part of Uzbekistan, near the border with Tajikistan. It is a natural oasis in the desert, with lush forests, waterfalls, lakes, and wildlife. It is also a cultural oasis, as it preserves the traditional way of life of the Nuratau people, who are descendants of Alexander the Great's soldiers. The Nuratau Mountains offer a variety of activities for travelers, such as hiking, camping, horse riding, fishing, and bird watching. They also offer a chance to experience the hospitality and culture of the Nuratau people, who live in eco-friendly guesthouses and share their customs and cuisine with visitors.

Chapter 2. Why Visit Uzbekistan?

Beyond the Tourist Hotspots

Uzbekistan has many lesser-known and off-the-beaten-path places and experiences that will make your trip more adventurous and authentic. Here are some of them:

Remote villages: Uzbekistan has many remote villages that are hidden in the mountains, deserts, or valleys. These villages offer a glimpse into the traditional and rural life of the Uzbek people, who still practice their ancient customs and crafts. Some of the villages that you can visit are Asraf in the Nuratau Mountains, which is famous for its pottery and carpets, Yangikazgan in the Kyzylkum Desert, which is a nomadic camp where you can stay in a yurt and ride a camel, and Margilan in the Fergana Valley, which is the center of silk production and weaving in Uzbekistan.

- Nomadic lifestyle: Uzbekistan has a nomadic heritage that dates back to the times of the Turkic tribes and the Mongol invasion. Many Uzbeks still live a nomadic or semi-nomadic lifestyle, especially in the desert and mountain regions. You can experience the nomadic lifestyle by staying in a yurt, which is a traditional tent made of felt and wood, eating the nomadic cuisine, such as kumis (fermented mare's milk) and shurpa (meat and vegetable soup), and participating in the nomadic activities, such as hunting with eagles or playing buzkashi (a game similar to polo but with a goat carcass).

Desert landscapes: Uzbekistan has some of the most spectacular and diverse desert landscapes in the world. The Kyzylkum Desert covers about 60% of the country's territory and is one of the largest deserts in the world. It has many attractions, such as the Aydarkul Lake, which is an artificial lake that was created by accident due to a dam breach, the Sarmysh Gorge, which is a rock art gallery that contains over 4,000 petroglyphs dating from the Paleolithic to the Middle Ages, and the Nurata Reserve, which is a wildlife sanctuary that hosts rare animals, such as the Bukhara deer and the Persian leopard.

Local festivals: Uzbekistan has many local festivals that celebrate its culture, history, and nature. Some of the festivals that you can attend are the Navruz Festival, which is the Persian New Year that marks the spring equinox and is celebrated with music, dance, food, and games, the Silk and Spices Festival, which is held in Bukhara and showcases the ancient crafts and traditions of Uzbekistan, such as silk weaving, carpet making, embroidery, pottery, and jewelry making, and the Boysun Bahori Festival, which is held in Boysun and preserves the pre-Islamic rituals and folklore of Uzbekistan.

Unique Cultural Experiences

Uzbekistan has many unique cultural experiences that travelers can enjoy. Here are some of the ways that travelers can immerse themselves in the Uzbek culture:

Learning the Uzbek language: Uzbek is the official language of Uzbekistan and is spoken by about 85% of the population. It is a Turkic language that has been influenced by Persian, Arabic, Russian, and other languages. Learning some basic Uzbek phrases and words can help travelers communicate with the locals and appreciate the culture better. Some of the common Uzbek greetings are salom (hello), rahmat (thank you), and xayr (goodbye). Some of the useful Uzbek words are plov (rice dish), chaikhana (tea house), and bazaar (market).

Tasting the Uzbek cuisine: Uzbek cuisine is one of the most delicious and diverse in Central Asia. It is influenced by various cuisines, such as Persian, Turkish, Mongolian, Russian, and Chinese. It is also characterized by its use of meat, rice, bread, vegetables, spices, and dairy products. Some of the must-try dishes are plov, which is a rice dish cooked with meat, carrots, onions, and raisins, samsa, which is a pastry filled with meat, cheese, or vegetables, shashlik, which is a skewered meat grilled over charcoal, and lagman, which is a noodle soup with meat and vegetables. Some of the popular drinks are green tea, which is served in a small bowl called piala, ayran, which is a salty yogurt drink, and kumis, which is a fermented mare's milk.

Staying in a traditional guesthouse: One of the best ways to experience Uzbek hospitality and culture is to stay in a traditional guesthouse or homestay. These are usually family-run establishments that offer cozy and comfortable rooms, homemade meals, and local activities. Some of the benefits of staying in a guesthouse are that travelers can interact with the hosts and learn about their lifestyle, customs, and traditions, enjoy the authentic Uzbek cuisine and specialties, and participate in some of the local activities, such as cooking classes, handicraft workshops, or folk music performances.

Participating in a cultural event: Uzbekistan has a rich and vibrant culture that is expressed through its music, dance, literature, art, crafts, festivals, and ceremonies. Travelers can participate in some of the cultural events that take place throughout the year and witness the diversity and beauty of Uzbek culture. Some of the events that travelers can attend are the Navruz Festival, which is the Persian New Year that marks the spring equinox and is celebrated with music, dance, food, and games, the Silk and Spices Festival, which is held in Bukhara and showcases the ancient crafts and traditions of Uzbekistan, such as silk weaving, carpet making, embroidery, pottery, and jewelry making, and the Boysun Bahori Festival, which is held in Boysun and preserves the pre-Islamic rituals and folklore of Uzbekistan.

Chapter 3. Planning Your Trip

Visa Requirements

If you're planning a journey to this fascinating destination, it's essential to acquaint yourself with the visa requirements for entering Uzbekistan. In this book, we provide a detailed breakdown of everything you need to know about these requirements, encompassing the various visa types, associated fees, durations of validity, and the application process.

Visa Varieties for Uzbekistan

Tourist Visa: Ideal for travelers embarking on tourism, sightseeing, or cultural exchange. You have the option of applying for either a single-entry or a multiple-entry tourist visa, permitting stays of up to 30 days per entry.

eVisa: An electronic visa that can be conveniently obtained online, sparing you a trip to an embassy or consulate. It's accessible for citizens of over 50 countries traveling to Uzbekistan for tourism or business, valid for 30 days from the date of issue, and allows for a single entry.

Transit Visa: Appropriate if you're merely passing through Uzbekistan en route to another destination. You can apply for a transit visa at the airport or a border crossing point, or in advance at an embassy or consulate. This visa permits a stay of up to 72 hours and a single entry.

Business Visa: Suited for those traveling to Uzbekistan for professional purposes such as work, trade, investment, or other business activities. It can be single-entry or multiple-entry, granting stays of up to 30 days per entry.

Student Visa: Designed for students or researchers in Uzbekistan. The application process typically involves acquiring an invitation letter from the host institution. This visa is valid for up to one year, with multiple entry privileges.

Visa Application Process for Uzbekistan

The application process for a visa to Uzbekistan hinges on the type of visa you require. Here's a general overview of the application steps for each visa category:

Tourist Visa:

- Apply at an Uzbekistan embassy or consulate in your country or region. Usually, you will require the following paperwork:

- A current passport that is at least six months out from the date of your intended arrival.

- A completed and signed visa application form.

- A passport-sized photo.

- A visa confirmation from a sponsor in Uzbekistan, such as a travel agency, hotel, or individual.

- A method of payment for the visa fee (e.g., cash, credit card, or bank transfer).

eVisa:

- Apply online through the eVisa portal. Usually, you'll require the following paperwork:

 - A digital copy of your passport's personal data page.

 - A passport-sized photo.

 - An email address.

 - A method of payment for the visa fee (e.g., credit card or PayPal).

Transit Visa:

- Apply for a transit visa at the airport or a border crossing point in Uzbekistan. Usually, you'll require the following paperwork:

- A passport that is currently valid and has at least six months remaining on it when you want to arrive.

- A completed and signed visa application form.

- A passport-sized photo.

- A ticket or confirmation of onward travel to a third country.

- A method of payment for the visa fee (e.g., cash or credit card).

Business Visa:

- Apply at an Uzbekistan embassy or consulate in your country or region. Usually, you'll require the following paperwork:

- A passport that is currently valid and has at least six months remaining on it when you want to arrive.

- A completed and signed visa application form.

- A passport-sized photo.

- An invitation letter from your business partner in Uzbekistan, approved by the Ministry of Foreign Affairs of Uzbekistan.

- A method of payment for the visa fee (e.g., cash, credit card, or bank transfer).

Student Visa:

- Apply at an Uzbekistan embassy or consulate in your country or region. Usually, you'll require the following paperwork:

- A passport that is currently valid and has at least six months remaining on it when you want to arrive.

- A completed and signed visa application form.

- A passport-sized photo.

- An invitation letter from your host institution in Uzbekistan, endorsed by the Ministry of Foreign Affairs of Uzbekistan.

- A method of payment for the visa fee (e.g., cash, credit card, or bank transfer).

It's essential to note that these are general requirements, and the specific documentation may vary depending on your nationality and the location of your application. To obtain precise information regarding the necessary documentation, refer to the official website of the Ministry of Foreign Affairs of Uzbekistan or the eVisa portal.

Best Time to Visit

The best time to visit Uzbekistan depends on your preferences and priorities, but generally speaking, the spring and autumn seasons are the most favorable and popular times to visit. Here are some of the factors that you should consider when choosing the best time to visit Uzbekistan:

Weather: Uzbekistan has a continental climate, with hot and dry summers and cold and snowy winters. The average annual temperature ranges from 10°C in the north to 16°C in the south. The spring season (March to May) and the autumn season (September to November) are the most pleasant and comfortable times to visit, as the weather is mild and sunny, with temperatures ranging from 15°C to 25°C. The summer season (June to August) is the hottest and driest time to visit, as the weather is scorching and arid, with temperatures reaching up to 40°C or more. The winter season (December to February) is the coldest and snowiest time to visit, as the weather is freezing and snowy, with temperatures dropping below zero.

Seasons: Uzbekistan has four distinct seasons, each with its own characteristics and attractions. The spring season is the time of renewal and celebration, as nature blooms and the people celebrate the Navruz Festival, which is the Persian New Year that marks the spring equinox. The spring season is also a good time to visit the mountains and valleys, as they are green and lush. The summer season is the time of heat and adventure, as the desert landscapes become more dramatic and challenging. The summer season is also a good time to visit the lakes and rivers, as they offer a refreshing escape from the heat. The autumn season is the time of harvest and color, as nature turns golden and red and the people celebrate the Silk and Spices Festival, which showcases the ancient crafts and traditions of Uzbekistan. The autumn season is also a good time to visit the ancient cities, as they are less crowded and more atmospheric. The winter season is the time of cold and snow, as nature becomes white and frosty and the people celebrate the New Year and Christmas holidays. The winter season is also a good time to visit the ski resorts, as they offer a fun and exciting winter sport experience.

Events: Uzbekistan has many events that celebrate its culture, history, and nature throughout the year. Among the events you can go to are:

Navruz Festival: This is the Persian New Year that marks the spring equinox and is celebrated with music, dance, food, and games. It is held in late March or early April in various locations across Uzbekistan.

Silk and Spices Festival: This is a festival that showcases the ancient crafts and traditions of Uzbekistan, such as silk weaving, carpet making, embroidery, pottery, and jewelry making. It is held in late May or early June in Bukhara.

Boysun Bahori Festival: This is a festival that preserves the pre-Islamic rituals and folklore of Uzbekistan. It is held in late April or early May in Boysun.

Independence Day: This is a national holiday that commemorates the independence of Uzbekistan from the Soviet Union in 1991. It is held on September 1st in **Tashkent.**

Sharq Taronalari Festival: This is an international music festival that features performers from various countries who play traditional music instruments. It is held in late August or early September in Samarkand.

Prices

Uzbekistan is a relatively affordable destination for travelers, but prices may vary depending on the season, location, and demand. Generally speaking, prices are higher during peak seasons (spring and autumn), especially in popular tourist destinations (such as Samarkand, Bukhara, Khiva), during major events (such as Navruz Festival or Silk and Spices Festival), or during holidays (such as New Year or Christmas). Prices are lower during off-peak seasons (summer and winter), especially in less visited destinations (such as Nukus, Termez, Nurata), during weekdays (rather than weekends), or during low seasons (such as January or February).

Chapter 4. Booking Flights

Choosing the Right Airport

In this guide, we introduce you to the primary airports in Uzbekistan, elucidating their locations, sizes, amenities, and connectivity. We also provide insightful tips to assist you in choosing the ideal airport for your destination and budget.

Tashkent International Airport (IATA: TAS, ICAO: UTTT) proudly claims the title of Uzbekistan's largest and busiest airport. Situated a mere 12 kilometers (7.5 miles) from the heart of Tashkent, the nation's capital and largest city, this airport houses two terminals: Terminal 2 for international flights and Terminal 3 for domestic flights. Serving as the primary hub for Uzbekistan Airways, the nation's flagship carrier, this airport offers an extensive network of flights to over 50 destinations across Asia, Europe, and the Middle East.

Tashkent International Airport caters to passengers with a range of amenities, including:

- Complimentary Wi-Fi.
- ATM facilities and currency exchange services.
- Duty-free shops and souvenir boutiques.
- An array of cafes and restaurants.
- Lounges and VIP services.
- A medical center and pharmacy.
- Luggage storage and lockers.
- Car rental and taxi services.
- Hotel accommodations and transit rooms.

Tashkent International Airport should top your list if:

- You intend to explore Tashkent or other Uzbek cities via domestic flights.
- You prefer a broader selection of flight options and international connections.
- You're comfortable with the hustle and bustle typically associated with major airports.

The second-largest airport in Uzbekistan, Samarkand International Airport (IATA: SKD, ICAO: UTSS): Is nestled approximately 6 kilometers (3.7 miles) from the heart of Samarkand, one of the nation's oldest and most renowned cities. Housing a single terminal serving both international and domestic flights, this airport functions as a secondary hub for Uzbekistan Airways. It also serves as the base for Somon Air, a private airline hailing from Tajikistan. Samarkand International Airport offers travelers access to more than 20 destinations spanning Asia, Europe, and the Middle East.

Samarkand International Airport caters to passengers with a range of amenities, including:

- Complimentary Wi-Fi.
- ATM facilities and currency exchange services.
- Duty-free shops and souvenir boutiques.
- An array of cafes and restaurants.
- Lounges and VIP services.
- A medical center and pharmacy.
- Luggage storage and lockers.
- Car rental and taxi services.

Samarkand International Airport is your best bet if:

- Your travel itinerary includes Samarkand or other historical cities in Uzbekistan via domestic flights.

- You prefer a shorter flight duration and a less congested airport when compared to Tashkent.
- You don't mind having fewer flight choices and international connections.

Bukhara International Airport (IATA: BHK, ICAO: UTSB) secures its position as Uzbekistan's third-largest airport, situated approximately 4 kilometers (2.5 miles) from the heart of Bukhara, another of the country's celebrated ancient cities. The airport boasts a single terminal serving both international and domestic flights. Uzbekistan Airways primarily operates out of this airport, alongside a few other airlines from Russia, Turkey, Iran, and Kazakhstan. Travelers can access more than 10 destinations across Asia and Europe.

Bukhara International Airport caters to passengers with a range of amenities, including:

- Complimentary Wi-Fi.
- ATM facilities and currency exchange services.
- Duty-free shops and souvenir boutiques.
- An array of cafes and restaurants.
- Lounges and VIP services.
- A medical center and pharmacy.
- Luggage storage and lockers.
- -lCar rental and taxi services.

Bukhara International Airport is the ideal choice if:

- You're planning to visit Bukhara or other culturally rich Uzbek cities via domestic flights.
- You seek a more authentic and traditional experience in Uzbekistan.
- You don't mind limited international flight options and connections.

Other Airports in Uzbekistan

Apart from the primary airports, Uzbekistan features several other airports primarily catering to domestic or regional flights to neighboring countries. A few of these airports include:

Fergana International Airport (IATA: FEG, ICAO: UTFF) in Fergana, a city nestled within the fertile Fergana Valley.

Navoi International Airport (IATA: NVI, ICAO: UTSA) in Navoiy, a city situated in the central region of Uzbekistan.

Nukus Airport (IATA: NCU, ICAO: UTNN) in Nukus, the capital of the autonomous republic of Karakalpakstan.

Urgench International Airport (IATA: UGC, ICAO: UTNU) in Urgench, a city in proximity to the renowned Khiva.

Consider these airports if:

- Your itinerary includes specific regions or cities in Uzbekistan with limited connectivity from other airports.
- You're yearning for an off-the-beaten-path adventure and are willing to embrace basic facilities and services at these airports.

Uzbekistan beckons travelers with its rich history, culture, and natural wonders. However, before you embark on your journey and book your flight, it's essential to select the airport that best suits your travel requirements. Depending on your priorities and preferences, you can opt for Tashkent, Samarkand, Bukhara, or one of the other airports in Uzbekistan. Each airport has its advantages, disadvantages, and unique charms. Regardless of your choice, we trust that this guide will assist you in planning a seamless and hassle-free trip to Uzbekistan.

Airlines and Flight Options

Choosing Airlines and Flight Options for Your Journey to Uzbekistan

We offer valuable tips to assist you in selecting the best airline or flight option that aligns with your comfort and convenience.

Uzbekistan Airways

Uzbekistan Airways, the national flag carrier of Uzbekistan, serves as the primary airline for the nation. Operating flights to more than 50 destinations across Asia, Europe, and the Middle East, it plays a pivotal role as the primary hub for Tashkent International Airport (TAS), Uzbekistan's largest and busiest airport. Notably, Uzbekistan Airways offers nonstop flights from London Heathrow (LHR) to Tashkent and connecting flights from various departure points via Istanbul (IST), Moscow (DME), or Dubai (DXB).

Uzbekistan Airways presents a spectrum of advantages and disadvantages for passengers:

Advantages:

- Direct flights from London to Tashkent, saving time and convenience.
- The UzAirPlus frequent flyer program, allowing passengers to accrue and redeem miles for flights, upgrades, and other benefits[2].
- The Bright Thursday promotion, offering discounts on online ticket purchases every Thursday[3].

Disadvantages:

- Limited network of destinations compared to other airlines, particularly in North America and Africa.
- A mixed reputation for service quality, safety, and punctuality.
- A relatively high rate of baggage loss and damage.

Uzbekistan Airways is your ideal choice if:

- You seek nonstop flights from London to Tashkent without layovers.
- The UzAirPlus program's miles and rewards appeal to you.

- Discounts through the Bright Thursday promotion align with your travel plans.

Turkish Airlines

As the national flag carrier of Turkey and one of the world's largest airlines, Turkish Airlines offers service to over 300 destinations across Asia, Europe, Africa, and the Americas. It serves as the central hub for Istanbul Airport (IST), a major European aviation hub. Turkish Airlines provides connecting flights to various Uzbek destinations, including Tashkent, Samarkand (SKD), Bukhara (BHK), and Fergana (FEG) via Istanbul.

Turkish Airlines boasts a range of advantages and disadvantages for travelers:

Advantages:

- Extensive flight options and connections to Uzbekistan compared to other carriers.
- The Miles&Smiles frequent flyer program, offering passengers the opportunity to earn and redeem miles for flights, upgrades, and other perks.
- A strong reputation for exceptional service quality, safety, and punctuality.

Disadvantages:

- Requirement of a layover in Istanbul, which may extend travel time.
- Relatively higher fares, particularly during peak seasons.
- Stringent visa requirements for transit passengers necessitating departure from Istanbul Airport.

Turkish Airlines is your preferred airline if:

- You value having a wide array of flight options and connections to Uzbekistan from multiple departure points.
- The Miles&Smiles program's mileage and rewards structure aligns with your travel preferences.
- Quality service and in-flight safety are paramount to your travel experience.

Tips for Finding Deals

Finding deals on flights to Uzbekistan can help you save money and enjoy your trip more. Here are some tips for finding deals on flights to Uzbekistan:

Booking in advance:

One of the best ways to find deals on flights to Uzbekistan is to book your tickets in advance, preferably at least two or three months before your departure date. Booking in advance can help you secure lower fares, better seats, and more availability. However, booking in advance may also limit your flexibility and options, as you may have to pay more fees or penalties if you want to change or cancel your booking.

Comparing prices:

Another way to find deals on flights to Uzbekistan is to compare prices and options of different airlines and flights. You can use online resources such as Skyscanner, Kayak, Expedia, or Hopper to compare prices and options of different airlines and flights. Comparing prices can help you find the best deals, discounts, or offers that suit your budget and preferences. However, comparing prices may also take more time and effort, as you may have to check multiple websites or apps and filter through various criteria and features.

Using discounts or coupons:

A third way to find deals on flights to Uzbekistan is to use discounts or coupons that are offered by various sources, such as airlines, travel agencies, credit cards, or loyalty programs. You can use discounts or coupons to reduce the cost of your tickets, get extra benefits or services, or earn rewards or points. However, using discounts or coupons may also require some conditions or limitations, such as minimum purchase, expiration date, or availability.

Being flexible:

A fourth way to find deals on flights to Uzbekistan is to be flexible with your travel dates, times, destinations, or routes. Being flexible can help you take advantage of lower fares, last-minute deals, or special offers that are available for certain periods or locations. However, being flexible may also involve some risks or inconveniences, such as changing plans, missing connections, or traveling longer.

Chapter 5. Getting to Know Uzbekistan

Diverse Landscapes and Regions

Uzbekistan is a country that has diverse landscapes and regions, each with its own characteristics and attractions. Here are some of the regions that you can visit in Uzbekistan:

Deserts:

Uzbekistan has two major deserts, the Kyzylkum and the Karakum, which cover about 80% of the country's territory. The deserts are mostly sandy and gravelly, with sparse vegetation and wildlife. The deserts are also rich in natural resources, such as gold, uranium, copper, and natural gas. One of the most remarkable features of the deserts is the Aral Sea, which was once the fourth largest lake in the world, but has shrunk dramatically since the 1960s due to irrigation projects that diverted water from its main sources, the Amu Darya and Syr Darya rivers. The Aral Sea is now divided into several smaller lakes, some of which are saline and toxic, while others are freshwater and support fishing and tourism. The Aral Sea disaster has caused severe environmental and social problems for the region, such as desertification, salinization, pollution, health issues, and economic decline. Visiting the deserts can be a challenging but rewarding experience, as you can witness the beauty and tragedy of nature, as well as the resilience and adaptation of the people.

Mountains:

Uzbekistan has two main mountain ranges, the Pamir and the Tien Shan, which are part of the Himalayan system and extend into Uzbekistan's southeastern corner. They are the highest mountains in Central Asia and include some of the world's highest peaks, such as Ismoil Somoni Peak (7,495 meters) and Lenin Peak (7,134 meters). The mountains are known for their glaciers, alpine lakes, and diverse flora and fauna. They are also home to some ethnic minorities, such as the Pamiris and the Wakhi. Visiting the mountains can be a thrilling and adventurous experience, as you can enjoy hiking, camping, horse riding, fishing, or skiing. You can also experience the culture and hospitality of the mountain people, who live in traditional houses and practice ancient religions.

Valleys:

Uzbekistan has several fertile and densely populated valleys that span across Uzbekistan, Kyrgyzstan, and Tajikistan. The most famous one is the Fergana Valley, which is surrounded by the Tien Shan Mountains in the north and the Pamir-Alai Mountains in the south. The Fergana Valley is one of the oldest and most important cultural centers of Central Asia, with a history dating back to ancient times. It is also one of the most ethnically diverse and politically sensitive areas of Uzbekistan, as it hosts various ethnic groups, such as Uzbeks, Tajiks, Kyrgyzs, Uyghurs, Russians, and others. Visiting the valleys can be a fascinating and enlightening experience, as you can explore the history and culture of Central Asia. You can also admire the natural beauty and diversity of the valleys, which are known for their fruits, flowers, and silk.

Lakes:

Uzbekistan has many lakes that offer a refreshing escape from the heat and dryness of the deserts or steppes. Some of the lakes are natural, while others are artificial or man-made. One of the most popular lakes is Aydar Lake, which is an artificial lake that was created by accident in 1969 due to a dam breach on the Syr Darya river. The lake covers an area of about 4,000 square kilometers and has a depth of about 15 meters. The lake is a popular destination for fishing, boating, swimming, or camping. Another lake that is worth visiting is Charvak Lake, which is a reservoir that was created in 1970 by damming the Chirchiq river. The lake covers an area of about 40 square kilometers and has a depth of about 40 meters. The lake is surrounded by green hills and forests and is a popular destination for water sports, hiking, or picnicking.

Local Traditions and Authentic Experiences

Uzbekistan has a rich and vibrant culture that reflects its diverse history and heritage. Uzbekistan is influenced by various religions, such as Zoroastrianism, Buddhism, Islam, Christianity, and Judaism. Uzbekistan is also influenced by various ethnic groups, such as Uzbeks, Tajiks, Kazakhs, Kyrgyzs, Turkmen, Karakalpaks, Russians, Koreans, and others. You can immerse yourself in Uzbek culture by participating in some of the local traditions and authentic experiences that Uzbekistan has to offer. Here are some of them:

Music:

Uzbek music is a fusion of Persian classical music and Central Asian folk music. One of the most famous genres of Uzbek music is Shashmaqam, which means "six modes" in Persian. Shashmaqam is a complex and sophisticated musical system that combines melodic, rhythmic, and poetic elements. Shashmaqam is performed by singers and instrumentalists who play traditional instruments, such as the tanbur (a long-necked lute), the doira (a frame drum), the nay (a reed flute), or the sato (a bowed lute). Shashmaqam is recognized by UNESCO as an Intangible Cultural Heritage of Humanity. Participating in the music tradition of Uzbekistan can help you learn more about the history and culture of the country, as well as enjoy the beauty and harmony of the music.

Dance:

Uzbek dance is a lively and expressive dance that originated from the Khorezm region. One of the most popular styles of Uzbek dance is Lazgi, which means "joyful" or "cheerful" in Turkic. Lazgi is a solo dance that involves fast and rhythmic movements of the head, shoulders, arms, and hips. Lazgi is usually performed by women who wear colorful dresses and scarves. Lazgi is often accompanied by upbeat music that features instruments such as the gijjak (a spike fiddle), the chang (a dulcimer), or the zurna (a double-reed pipe). Participating in the dance tradition of Uzbekistan can help you have fun and express yourself, as well as appreciate the diversity and creativity of the dance.

Literature:

Uzbek literature is one of the oldest and most influential literatures in Central Asia. It has a long and rich tradition that spans over a thousand years. One of the most prominent figures of Uzbek literature is Alisher Navoiy, who is considered one of the greatest poets of Central Asia. Navoiy was born in 1441 in Herat, which was then part of the Timurid Empire. He wrote in both Persian and Chagatai Turkic, which was the ancestor of modern Uzbek language. He composed many works of poetry, prose, and criticism that expressed his humanistic and mystical views. He also contributed to the development and promotion of the Chagatai Turkic language and literature. Navoiy is revered as a national hero and a cultural icon in Uzbekistan. Participating in the literature tradition of Uzbekistan can help you improve your language skills and critical thinking, as well as admire the wisdom and elegance of the literature.

Art:

Uzbek art is a form of visual expression that reflects the diverse influences and styles of Uzbekistan. One of the most distinctive forms of Uzbek art is Suzani embroidery, which means "needlework" in Persian. Suzani embroidery is a form of needlework that uses colorful silk threads to create floral or geometric patterns on cotton or silk fabric. Suzani embroidery is usually made by women who use it as a form of decoration or dowry. Suzani embroidery can be found on various items, such as wall hangings, bed covers, tablecloths, or cushions. Suzani embroidery is also regarded as a symbol of fertility and prosperity. Participating in the art tradition of Uzbekistan can help you develop your artistic skills and creativity, as well as appreciate the beauty and diversity of the art.

Crafts:

Uzbek crafts are a form of material culture that showcases the ancient skills and techniques of Uzbekistan. Some of the most common types of Uzbek crafts are pottery, carpet making, metalworking, leatherworking, or wood carving. Pottery is one of the oldest forms of Uzbek crafts that dates back to prehistoric times. Pottery is made by shaping clay into various forms and firing it in a kiln. Pottery can be used for various purposes, such as cooking, storing, serving, or decorating. Pottery can also be painted or glazed with various colors and designs. Carpet making is another form of Uzbek crafts that involves weaving woolen threads into intricate patterns on a loom. Carpet making can be traced back to the nomadic tribes who used carpets for warmth and comfort. Carpets can also be used for various purposes, such as flooring, wall hanging, or prayer mat. Metalworking is another form of Uzbek crafts that involves shaping metal into various objects, such as jewelry, coins, weapons, or utensils. Metalworking can be done by using various methods, such as casting, forging, hammering, or engraving. Metalworking can also be decorated with various techniques, such as inlaying, gilding, or enameling. Leatherworking is another form of Uzbek crafts that involves processing animal skins into various products, such as bags, shoes, belts, or hats. Leatherworking can be done by using various methods, such as tanning, dyeing, cutting, or stitching. Leatherworking can also be decorated with various techniques, such as embossing, stamping, or painting. Wood carving is another form of Uzbek crafts that involves cutting wood into various shapes and patterns. Wood carving can be used for various purposes, such as furniture, doors, windows, or musical instruments. Wood carving can also be painted or lacquered with various colors and designs. Participating in the crafts tradition of Uzbekistan can help you learn more about the history and culture of the country, as well as enjoy the craftsmanship and quality of the crafts.

Festivals:

Uzbek festivals are a form of social and cultural celebration that mark various occasions and events in Uzbekistan. Some of the most popular festivals are Nowruz, Silk and Spices Festival, Boysun Bahori Festival, and Independence Day. Nowruz is the Persian New Year that marks the spring equinox and is celebrated with music, dance, food, and games. It is held in late March or early April in various locations across Uzbekistan. Silk and Spices Festival is a festival that showcases the ancient crafts and traditions of Uzbekistan, such as silk weaving, carpet making, embroidery, pottery, and jewelry making. It is held in late May or early June in Bukhara. Boysun Bahori Festival is a festival that preserves the pre-Islamic rituals and folklore of Uzbekistan. It is held in late April or early May in Boysun. Independence Day is a national holiday that commemorates the independence of Uzbekistan from the Soviet Union in 1991. It is held on September 1st in Tashkent. Participating in the festivals of Uzbekistan can help you have fun and socialize with the locals, as well as experience the diversity and vibrancy of the culture.

Ceremonies:

Uzbek ceremonies are a form of ritual and symbolic action that express various values and beliefs in Uzbekistan. Some of the most common ceremonies are weddings, funerals, births, or circumcisions. Weddings are one of the most important and elaborate ceremonies in Uzbekistan that involve various stages and customs. Some of the stages are matchmaking, engagement, henna night, wedding day, and walima (reception). Some of the customs are exchanging gifts, wearing traditional clothes, singing songs, dancing dances, eating food, or giving blessings. Funerals are another important ceremony in Uzbekistan that involve various stages and customs. Some of the stages are washing the body, wrapping the body in a shroud, carrying the body to the cemetery, burying the body in a grave, reciting prayers, or visiting the grave. Some of the customs are wearing black clothes, expressing condolences, giving charity, or offering food. Births are another important ceremony in Uzbekistan that involve various stages and customs. Some of the stages are pregnancy, delivery, naming, or circumcision. Some of the customs are celebrating with family and friends, giving gifts, performing rituals, or reading verses. Circumcisions are another important ceremony in Uzbekistan that involve various stages and customs. Some of the stages are choosing a date, inviting guests, preparing the child, or performing the operation. Some of the customs are dressing the child in white clothes, playing music, giving sweets, or congratulating the parents. Participating in the ceremonies of Uzbekistan can help you respect and understand the values and beliefs of the people, as well as appreciate the symbolism and significance of the ceremonies.

Chapter 6. Exploring Uzbekistan's Cities

Tashkent The Capital

Tashkent is the largest and most populous city in Uzbekistan, as well as the political, economic, and cultural center of the country. Tashkent has a long and varied history, dating back to ancient times when it was a part of various empires and kingdoms. Today, Tashkent is a modern and cosmopolitan city that offers a range of attractions and landmarks for visitors to enjoy.

Some of the main attractions and landmarks of Tashkent are:

1. The Amir Timur Square, which is the heart of the city and features a statue of Amir Timur, the founder of the Timurid Empire, as well as a museum dedicated to his life and achievements.

2. The Chorsu Bazaar, which is one of the oldest and largest markets in Central Asia, where you can find a variety of goods, such as spices, fruits, vegetables, handicrafts, carpets, and souvenirs.

3. The Kukeldash Madrasah, which is a 16th-century Islamic school that is now a museum and a mosque. It is one of the most impressive examples of medieval architecture in Tashkent.

4. The Tashkent Tower, which is the tallest structure in Central Asia, standing at 375 meters high. It offers a panoramic view of the city and its surroundings, as well as a revolving restaurant and an observation deck.

5. The Tashkent Metro, which is not only a convenient and cheap way to get around the city, but also a showcase of artistic and cultural heritage. Each station has its own unique design and theme, featuring mosaics, sculptures, paintings, and chandeliers.

Samarkand - The Pearl of the Orient

Samarkand is one of the oldest and most famous cities in Central Asia, and it is often called the Pearl of the Orient. Samarkand is a city that showcases the beauty and splendor of Islamic architecture, as well as the influence of various civilizations and religions that have left their mark on its history.

Some of the architectural wonders of Samarkand are:

1. The Registan Square, which is the most iconic and majestic sight in Samarkand. It is a large public square surrounded by three stunning madrasas, or Islamic schools, that date back to the 15th and 17th centuries. The madrasas are decorated with intricate tile work, domes, minarets, and arches, creating a harmonious and symmetrical composition.

2. The Bibi-Khanym Mosque, which is one of the largest and most impressive mosques in Central Asia. It was built by Timur, the founder of the Timurid Empire, in the 14th century as a tribute to his wife, Bibi-Khanym. The mosque has a colossal dome, four towering minarets, and a spacious courtyard. The mosque also features a marble Quran stand that is said to have been carved by Bibi-Khanym herself.

3. The Shah-i-Zinda necropolis, which is a complex of mausoleums and tombs that house the remains of Timur's relatives, nobles, and saints. The

necropolis is located on a sacred hill where, according to legend, the cousin of Prophet Muhammad, Qusam ibn Abbas, was buried alive after spreading Islam in the region. The necropolis is a masterpiece of art and craftsmanship, with each mausoleum having its own unique design and decoration.

Samarkand is a city that has witnessed and shaped the history and culture of Central Asia for millennia. It is a city that offers a glimpse into the past, as well as a vibrant and lively present.

Bukhara - The Holy City

Bukhara is a city that has been a center of Islamic learning and scholarship for centuries. It is also known as the Holy City, because it has over 100 mosques, 50 madrasas, and 20 mausoleums, as well as numerous shrines and tombs of saints and scholars. Bukhara is a UNESCO World Heritage Site that preserves the rich and diverse heritage of Central Asian Islam.

Some of the mosques, madrasas, mausoleums, and bazaars that make Bukhara a unique and captivating city are:

1. The Kalyan Mosque, which is the second largest mosque in Central Asia, after the Bibi-Khanym Mosque in Samarkand. It can accommodate up to 12,000 worshippers and has a magnificent courtyard with 288 domes and 208 pillars.

2. The Mir-i-Arab Madrasa, which is one of the most important and influential Islamic schools in Central Asia. It was founded in the 16th century by Sheikh Abdullah Yamani, who was also known as Mir-i-Arab, or the Prince of Arabs. The madrasa has produced many prominent scholars and leaders, such as Imam Bukhari, the compiler of the most authentic collection of hadiths.

3. The Ismail Samani Mausoleum, which is the oldest and most elegant monument in Bukhara. It was built in the 10th century as the tomb of Ismail Samani, the founder of the Samanid dynasty, which was the first native Persian dynasty to rule Central Asia after the Arab conquest. The mausoleum is a masterpiece of brickwork and geometric patterns, reflecting the influence of Zoroastrianism and Buddhism on Islamic art.

4. The Lyab-i Hauz, which is a complex of buildings surrounding a large pond that dates back to the 17th century. It consists of two madrasas, a khanqah, or a Sufi lodge, and a statue of Nasreddin Hodja, a legendary folk hero and humorist. The Lyab-i Hauz is a popular place for locals and tourists to relax and enjoy the atmosphere of old Bukhara.

5. The Silk Road Bazaar, which is a colorful and lively market that sells a variety of goods, such as silk, carpets, ceramics, jewelry, spices, and dried fruits. The bazaar is located along the ancient trade route that connected China with Europe and the Middle East. The bazaar is a great place to experience the culture and cuisine of Bukhara.

Bukhara is a city that has a lot to offer for anyone who is interested in history, culture, or religion. It is a city that has been shaped by many civilizations and traditions, but has also maintained its own identity and character.

Khiva - The Museum City

Khiva is a city that transports you to the past, as it is a well-preserved medieval city that was once a powerful khanate and a major stop on the Silk Road. Khiva's old town, also known as Ichan-Kala, is a UNESCO World Heritage Site that contains more than 50 historical monuments and 250 old houses within its walls.

Some of the features and attractions of Khiva's old town are:

1. The walls, which are made of clay and date back to the 10th century. They are about 10 meters high and 6 meters thick, and have four gates that face the cardinal directions. The walls enclose an area of about 26 hectares, creating a sense of isolation and mystery.

2. The gates, which are the main entrances to the old town. They are named after the directions they face: Ata Darvaza (West Gate), Palvan Darvaza (East Gate), Tash Darvaza (South Gate), and Bogcha Darvaza (North Gate). Each gate has its own distinctive design and decoration, such as arches, towers, and inscriptions.

3. The palaces, which are the residences of the khans, or rulers, of Khiva. The most famous palace is the Kunya Ark, or Old Citadel, which was built in the 12th century and expanded over time. The Kunya Ark has several buildings, such

as a throne room, a mosque, a harem, a mint, and a prison. Another palace is the Tash Khauli, or Stone Palace, which was built in the 19th century and has a lavish courtyard with carved wooden columns and colorful tiles.

4. The minarets, which are the towers that call for prayer and symbolize the religious authority of Khiva. The most iconic minaret is the Kalta Minor, or Short Minaret, which was intended to be the tallest minaret in Central Asia, but was left unfinished due to the death of its patron. The Kalta Minor is covered with blue and green tiles and stands at 26 meters high. Another minaret is the Islam Khoja Minaret, which is the tallest minaret in Khiva, at 45 meters high. It has a slender shape and a spiral pattern of bricks and tiles.

5. The museums, which are housed in some of the historical buildings, display various aspects of Khiva's culture and history. Some of the museums are:
- The Allakuli Khan Madrasa, which is a 19th-century Islamic school that now serves as a museum of applied arts. It exhibits carpets,

ceramics, metalwork, embroidery, and jewelry from different regions of Uzbekistan.

- The Muhammad Rakhim Khan Madrasa, which is another 19th-century Islamic school that now serves as a museum of literature and history. It showcases manuscripts, books, documents, photographs, and personal belongings of Muhammad Rakhim Khan II, who was a poet and a reformer.

- The Juma Mosque, which is a 10th-century mosque that now serves as a museum of wood carving. It features 212 wooden pillars that support the roof and have intricate carvings of floral and geometric motifs.

Khiva is a city that offers a glimpse into the past, as well as a vibrant and lively present. It is a city that has a lot to offer for anyone who is interested in history, culture, or architecture.

Nukus and the Savitsky Museum

Nukus, the capital city of the autonomous republic of Karakalpakstan in northwestern Uzbekistan, might not be a tourist hotspot, but it holds unique significance. With a population of around 300,000 residents, Nukus is perched near the Aral Sea, a once-thriving body of water tragically impacted by environmental degradation. Its climate features hot, arid summers and cold, snowy winters.

While Nukus serves as the center of the cotton and textile industry in Karakalpakstan, it's also known for the presence of institutions like Karakalpak State University and the Karakalpak Philharmonic Orchestra.

The crown jewel of Nukus is the Savitsky Museum, also known as the Nukus Museum of Art or the Museum of Forbidden Art. Founded in 1966 by Igor Savitsky, an electrician, archaeologist, and art enthusiast, this museum is home to a vast collection of Russian and Central Asian avant-garde artworks. These works, considered unconventional and experimental by the Soviet authorities, were saved from censorship and persecution because Nukus was distantly removed from the watchful eyes of Moscow and Tashkent.

Beyond art, the museum houses an assortment of archaeological and ethnographic artifacts from Karakalpakstan, including pottery, carpets, jewelry, and costumes. The Savitsky Museum boasts one of the world's most extensive collections of Russian avant-garde art, second only to the Russian Museum in Saint Petersburg. With over 82,000 items in its treasury, ranging from paintings and sculptures to textiles, it showcases pieces by famous artists like Alexander Volkov, Mikhail Kurzin, Robert Falk, Vera Mukhina, and Vladimir Lysenko.

The museum not only celebrates art but also sheds light on the history and culture of Karakalpakstan, often hosting temporary exhibitions of contemporary art. Its cultural significance is underscored by UNESCO, which recognizes it as an Intangible Cultural Heritage of Humanity. The Savitsky Museum has even earned the moniker "the Louvre of Uzbekistan" by The Guardian, underlining its global acclaim.

While the Savitsky Museum is a remarkable cultural attraction in Nukus, the city itself offers a unique glimpse into an autonomous region within Uzbekistan, characterized by its own traditions, history, and contributions to the nation's heritage.

Termez and the Mausoleum of Al-Hakim

Termez is a city in the south of Uzbekistan, near the border with Afghanistan. It is one of the oldest and most important cities in Central Asia, with a history dating back to the 3rd century BC. Termez was a major center of trade, culture, and religion, as it was located on the crossroads of the Silk Road and the Oxus River. Termez was influenced by various civilizations, such as the Greeks, the Kushans, the Sassanids, the Arabs, the Mongols, the Timurids, and the Russians. Termez is also a city of diverse faiths, as it was home to Zoroastrians, Buddhists, Christians, Jews, and Muslims. Termez has many historical and cultural monuments that reflect its rich heritage, such as the Buddhist stupa of Fayaz Tepe, the Christian church of Dalverzin Tepe, the Jewish cemetery of Kara Tepe, and the Islamic mausoleum of Sultan Saodat.

The main attraction of Termez is the Mausoleum of Al-Hakim, which is also known as the Mausoleum of Hakim at-Termizi or Termez-ota. Al-Hakim was a famous Islamic scholar, mystic, and saint who lived in the 9th century. He was the founder of the Hakimiyya order of Sufism and the author of many works on theology and philosophy. He was also a friend and teacher of Imam al-Bukhari, who compiled one of the most authoritative collections of hadiths (sayings of

Prophet Muhammad). Al-Hakim died in Termez in 869 and was buried in a simple grave. Over time, his grave became a popular place of pilgrimage and a mausoleum was built over it. The mausoleum is considered to be one of the most sacred and beautiful monuments in Uzbekistan. The mausoleum has a dome-shaped structure made of brick and decorated with carved marble and glazed tiles. The mausoleum has a marble tombstone with an inscription that praises Al-Hakim's virtues and achievements. The mausoleum also has a mosque, a library, and a museum that display some of Al-Hakim's manuscripts and relics. The mausoleum is recognized by UNESCO as an Intangible Cultural Heritage of Humanity.

Andijan and the Babur Park

Andijan is a city in the east of Uzbekistan, near the border with Kyrgyzstan. It is one of the oldest and largest cities in the Fergana Valley, with a population of about 400,000 people. Andijan is known for its industry, education, and culture. Andijan is the center of the automotive and textile industry in Uzbekistan, as it hosts the GM Uzbekistan plant and several cotton factories. Andijan is also the home of the Andijan State University and the Andijan Medical Institute, which are among the leading educational institutions in the country. Andijan is also a city of diverse faiths and ethnicities, as it hosts various mosques, churches, synagogues, and temples, as well as Uzbeks, Kyrgyzs, Tajiks, Russians, Koreans, and others.

The main attraction of Andijan is the Babur Park, which is a memorial park dedicated to Zahiriddin Muhammad Babur, the founder of the Mughal Empire in India and a great poet and commander. Babur was born in Andijan in 1483 and ruled the city until he left for India in 1526. Babur Park was established in 1993 on the Bogishamol hill, where Babur used to have a summerhouse and a garden. The park includes a house museum that displays some of Babur's manuscripts, relics, and portraits. The park also features a statue of Babur on a horse, which was erected on the central square of Andijan in 1970. The park also has a symbolic tomb of Babur, which contains soil from Agra and Kabul, where Babur died and was buried. The park is surrounded by trees and flowers that create a picturesque and peaceful atmosphere. The park is visited by many admirers of Babur's work and legacy, as well as pilgrims who perform rituals to honor his memory.

Chapter 7 Historical and Architectural Marvels

Registan Square

Registan Square is the most iconic and majestic sight in Samarkand, the ancient capital of the Timurid Empire. It is a large public square surrounded by three stunning madrasas, or Islamic schools, that date back to the 15th and 17th centuries. The madrasas are:

1. The Ulugbek Madrasa, which was built by Ulugbek, the grandson of Timur and a famous astronomer and mathematician. It has a blue-tiled facade with a large arch and two minarets. The entrance is decorated with stars and geometric patterns, reflecting Ulugbek's interest in science.

2. The Sher-Dor Madrasa, which was built by Yalangtush Bahadur, the ruler of Samarkand in the 17th century. It has a yellow-tiled facade with a large arch and two minarets. The entrance is adorned with images of lions and deer, as well as suns with human faces, which are unusual motifs in Islamic art.

3. The Tilya-Kori Madrasa, which was also built by Yalangtush Bahadur, as part of his plan to complete the ensemble of the square. It has a golden-tiled facade with a large arch and two minarets. The entrance leads to a mosque and a

dome hall, which are covered with gold leaf and paintings.

Registan Square is a masterpiece of architecture and art, as well as a symbol of the cultural and intellectual achievements of the Timurid era.

Shah-i-Zinda Complex

Shah-i-Zinda Complex is a complex of mausoleums and tombs that house the remains of Timur's relatives, nobles, and saints. It is located on a sacred hill in Samarkand, where, according to legend, the cousin of Prophet Muhammad, Qusam ibn Abbas, was buried alive after spreading Islam in the region. The name of the complex means "The Living King", referring to Qusam ibn Abbas, who is believed to be still alive in an underground chamber.

Shah-i-Zinda Complex is not only a religious and historical site, but also a showcase of the artistic and cultural diversity of Central Asian Islam. The complex consists of more than 20 mausoleums that date from the 11th to the 19th centuries. Each mausoleum has its own unique design and decoration, featuring various styles and influences, such as Persian, Mongol, Indian, and Chinese. The mausoleums are adorned with exquisite tile work, domes, arches, and carvings, creating a stunning visual effect.

Shah-i-Zinda Complex is a place that attracts pilgrims, tourists, and admirers of art and architecture from all over the world. It is a place that offers a glimpse into the past, as well as a reflection of the present.

Some of the most notable mausoleums are:

- The Shodi Mulk Oko Mausoleum, which is the oldest mausoleum in the complex. It was built in the 11th century for Shodi Mulk Oko, a princess of the Qarakhanid dynasty. It has a simple brick dome and a carved wooden door.

- The Qusam ibn Abbas Mausoleum, which is the most sacred mausoleum in the complex. It was built in the 14th century for Qusam ibn Abbas, the cousin of Prophet Muhammad. It has a blue-tiled dome and a marble sarcophagus.
- The Truman Aka Mausoleum, which is one of the most beautiful mausoleums in the complex. It was built in the 15th century for Tuman Aka, the sister of Timur's wife. It has a turquoise-tiled

dome and a richly decorated interior with floral and geometric motifs.

Ark Fortress

Ark Fortress, a grand citadel situated in the northwestern part of Bukhara, carries with it centuries of history. Its origins trace back to the 5th century AD, making it a venerable relic of Bukhara's past. This colossal fortress served as both the political and military nerve center of Bukhara, alongside being a hub for culture and religion. For ages, it stood as the formidable residence and stronghold of the city's rulers, until the fortress succumbed to Russian forces in 1920.

Within the fortress walls lie several captivating buildings and museums, each with its own unique narrative:

1. The throne room, an opulent chamber where emirs of Bukhara welcomed guests and conducted ceremonies. Its grandeur is exemplified by a high ceiling, a marble floor, and a resplendent wooden throne adorned with gold and precious stones.

2. The reception and coronation court, a place where emirs marked their ascent to the throne and received foreign envoys. It boasts a spacious hall crowned with a dome, a graceful balcony, and a charming fountain.

3. The local history museum, a treasure trove of artifacts and exhibits that delve into the rich tapestry of Bukhara's history and culture. The museum is divided into sections dedicated to archaeology, ethnography, numismatics, weaponry, costumes, and jewelry.

4. The court mosque, a serene space where emirs and their courtiers would gather for prayer. It features an unassuming design with a mihrab, a minbar, and a wooden ceiling.

Itchan Kala

Itchan Kala, the ancient heart of Khiva, is a mesmerizing step back in time. This remarkably well-preserved medieval city once reigned as a powerful khanate and a vital stop along the Silk Road. As a UNESCO World

Heritage Site, Itchan Kala houses over 50 historical landmarks and 250 ancient houses within its storied walls.

Some of the most captivating features and attractions within Itchan Kala include:

1. The Walls: These clay fortifications, harking back to the 10th century, are a robust testament to the city's history. Standing at approximately 10 meters in height and 6 meters in thickness, they feature four cardinal-facing gates, encapsulating an area of roughly 26 hectares, shrouding the enclave in an aura of seclusion and intrigue.

2. The Gates: Serving as the primary entry points to the old town, Itchan Kala's gates are named after the directions they face: Ata Darvaza (West Gate), Palvan Darvaza (East Gate), Tash Darvaza (South Gate), and Bogcha Darvaza (North Gate). Each gate boasts a unique design and ornate decorations, such as arches, towers, and inscriptions.

3. The Palaces: The residences of Khiva's khans or rulers are a sight to behold. The renowned Kunya Ark, or Old Citadel, constructed in the 12th century and expanded over time, houses several buildings, including a throne room, a mosque, a harem, a mint, and a prison. Another gem is the Tash Khauli, or Stone Palace, which dates back to the 19th century and boasts a sumptuous courtyard adorned with intricately carved wooden columns and vibrant tiles.

4. The Minarets: These towering structures, which summon the faithful to prayer, are symbols of Khiva's religious heritage. The most iconic is the Kalta Minor, or Short Minaret, covered in blue and green tiles, standing at 26 meters high. Another remarkable minaret is the Islam Khoja Minaret, Khiva's tallest at 45 meters, distinguished by its slender form and a mesmerizing spiral pattern of bricks and tiles.

5. The Museums: Scattered across historical buildings, these museums showcase various facets of Khiva's culture and history. Notable museums include the Allakuli Khan Madrasa, which houses a collection of applied arts, and the Muhammad Rakhim Khan Madrasa, serving as a

repository of literature and history. Additionally, the Juma Mosque, a 10th-century marvel, has been transformed into a museum of wood carving, featuring 212 intricately carved wooden pillars supporting the roof.

Chapter 8 Arts and Crafts

Suzani Embroidery

Introduction:

Suzani embroidery, a cherished form of needlework hailing from Central Asia, is a tapestry of tradition, culture, and symbolism. The word "suzani" finds its roots in the Persian word "sozan," which means needle. This art form, characterized by its vibrant colors and intricate patterns, reflects the desires and wishes of the talented artisans who create it. In this blog post, we will delve into the fascinating world of suzani embroidery, exploring its origin, production process, symbolism, and the occasions where it takes center stage.

Origin and Meaning:

The term "suzani" is intrinsically tied to the Persian word "sozan" or "suzan," which signifies needlework. This etymological connection highlights the craft's long standing association with Persian culture and its central role in Central Asian societies. Suzani embroidery is particularly prominent in Uzbekistan, Tajikistan, Kazakhstan, and Turkmenistan.

Production Process:

Suzani embroidery is a labor-intensive craft that requires skill and patience. Artisans typically use handwoven cotton or silk fabric as a canvas for their creations. Threads are dyed using natural pigments to achieve the vibrant colors suzani is known for. Embroiderers employ a variety of stitches, such as chain, satin, and buttonhole stitches, to create intricate patterns and motifs. Common motifs include sun and moon symbols, pomegranates, flowers, and geometric designs.

Colors and Materials:

Suzani embroidery is celebrated for its rich, bold color palette, with shades of red, blue, green, and gold taking center stage. These colors not only represent the region's vibrant culture but also hold specific meanings. For instance, red symbolizes life and the sun, while blue often represents water and spirituality. Gold accents are indicative of wealth and prosperity.

Cultural and Symbolic Significance:

Suzani embroidery is more than just a form of artistic expression; it carries deep cultural and symbolic meaning. It is often associated with wishes and desires for a better life. Many artisans incorporate motifs like the

"Tree of Life," signifying fertility and abundance, into their work. The art of suzani allows individuals to channel their aspirations and hopes into a tangible form, reflecting a wish for a prosperous and harmonious future.

Occasions and Display:

Suzani embroidery plays a central role in various life events and celebrations. It is frequently used as a part of dowries, symbolizing a bride's future happiness and prosperity. Suzani textiles are also used as wall hangings, tablecloths, and bedcovers to decorate homes during weddings, festivals, and other significant occasions. The intricate patterns and vibrant colors of suzani embroidery add a touch of elegance to these events, reflecting the cultural richness of Central Asia.

Conclusion:

Suzani embroidery is a cherished tradition that has stood the test of time, bridging cultures and generations in Central Asia. Its deep-rooted symbolism, vibrant colors, and intricate designs continue to enchant people around the world. Suzani embroidery is not merely a craft; it is a testament to the hopes and dreams of the artisans who bring it to life, making it a cultural treasure worth celebrating and preserving.

Ceramic and Pottery

Ceramic and pottery are two terms that are often used interchangeably, but they have different meanings. Ceramic is a general term that refers to any product made from clay or other non-metallic minerals that has been shaped and hardened by heat. Pottery is a specific type of ceramic that is made from clay that has been molded and fired at low temperatures, usually below 1200°C. Pottery is one of the oldest and most widespread forms of ceramic art, and it can be used for functional or decorative purposes.

If you want to learn about ceramic and pottery, here are some basic steps that you need to follow:

1. Preparing the clay: The first step is to prepare the clay that you will use for your ceramic or pottery project. You can either buy ready-made clay from a store or make your own clay from natural materials. You need to knead the clay to remove any air bubbles and make it smooth and pliable. You also need to adjust the moisture level of the clay by adding water or letting it dry until it reaches the desired consistency.

2. Shaping the clay: The next step is to shape the clay into the form that you want. You can use different methods to shape the clay, such as hand-building, wheel-throwing, slab-rolling, molding, or extruding. Hand-building involves using your hands and simple tools to create shapes from coils, balls, or slabs of clay. Wheel-throwing involves using a rotating wheel to shape the clay into symmetrical forms, such as bowls, cups, or vases. Slab-rolling involves using a rolling pin or a machine to flatten the clay into thin sheets that can be cut and joined together. Molding involves using a hollow container or a carved object to press the clay into a specific shape. Extruding involves forcing the clay through a nozzle or a die to create tubes, rods, or other shapes.

3. Firing the clay: The third step is to fire the clay in a kiln, which is a special oven that can reach high temperatures. Firing the clay makes it hard and durable, and also changes its color and texture. There are different types of firing, such as bisque firing, glaze firing, or raku firing. Bisque firing is the first firing that removes any remaining water from the clay and makes it porous and ready for glazing. Glaze firing is the second firing that

melts the glaze onto the surface of the clay and creates a shiny and colorful coating. Raku firing is a special type of firing that involves removing the hot pottery from the kiln and placing it in a container with combustible materials, such as paper or sawdust, to create crackled effects and metallic colors.

4. Glazing the clay: The fourth step is to glaze the clay, which is optional but recommended for enhancing the appearance and durability of your ceramic or pottery. Glaze is a thin layer of glass-like material that can be applied to the surface of the clay before or after firing. Glaze can be transparent, opaque, matte, glossy, smooth, textured, or colored. Glaze can also protect your ceramic or pottery from water, stains, scratches, or chemicals.

5. Decorating the clay: The final step is to decorate your ceramic or pottery with various techniques, such as painting, stamping, carving, incising, sgraffito, slip trailing, or decals. Painting involves using brushes or pens to apply colors or designs on the surface of the clay. Stamping involves using objects with patterns or textures to imprint marks on the surface of the clay. Carving

involves using knives or tools to cut away parts of the clay to create relief effects. Incising involves using needles or tools to draw lines or shapes on the surface of the clay. Sgraffito involves scratching through a layer of colored slip (liquid clay) to reveal another color underneath. Slip trailing involves squeezing slip through a nozzle to create raised lines or dots on the surface of the clay. Decals involve transferring images from paper onto the surface of the clay. Decals involve transferring images from paper onto the clay using water or heat.

Some of the tools and equipment that you will need for ceramic and pottery are:

1. A kiln: A kiln is a device that heats up the clay to high temperatures and transforms it into ceramic or pottery. Kilns can be electric, gas, or wood-fired, and they come in different sizes and shapes. You can either buy a kiln, rent a kiln, or use a community kiln.

2. A wheel: A wheel is a device that rotates the clay and allows you to shape it into symmetrical forms. Wheels can be manual or electric, and

they have different parts, such as the head, the bat, the foot pedal, and the splash pan. You can either buy a wheel, rent a wheel, or use a community wheel.

3. A slab roller: A slab roller is a device that flattens the clay into thin sheets that can be cut and joined together. Slab rollers can be manual or electric, and they have different parts, such as the rollers, the crank, the canvas, and the table. You can either buy a slab roller, rent a slab roller, or use a community slab roller.

4. A mold: A mold is a container or an object that gives shape to the clay. Molds can be made of plaster, wood, metal, plastic, or other materials. You can either buy molds, make your own molds, or use found objects as molds.

5. A cutter: A cutter is a tool that cuts the clay into pieces or shapes. Cutters can be knives, scissors, cookie cutters, wire tools, or other sharp objects. You can either buy cutters, make your own cutters, or use found objects as cutters.

6. A brush: A brush is a tool that applies glaze or paint to the surface of the clay. Brushes can be made of hair, bristles, foam, or other materials. They can have different shapes and sizes, such as round, flat, fan, liner, etc. You can either buy brushes, make your own brushes, or use found objects as brushes.

Some tips and advice on how to improve your skills and creativity in ceramic and pottery are:

- Experiment with different types of clay, glazes, colors, textures, and techniques. Try to mix and match different elements and see what results you get.
- Learn from other ceramicists and potters. Watch videos, read books, take classes, join clubs, visit studios, attend exhibitions, or follow online communities. Observe how they work and what they create.
- Practice regularly and consistently. The more you work with clay, the more familiar and comfortable you will become with it. The more you fire your clay, the more you will understand how it behaves in the kiln. The more you glaze your clay,

Chapter 9. Outdoor Adventures Beyond the Obvious

Hiking in the Nuratau-Kyzylkum Biosphere Reserve

Hiking in the Nuratau-Kyzylkum Biosphere Reserve is one of the best ways to experience the natural and cultural diversity of Uzbekistan. The biosphere reserve covers an area of about 5,000 square kilometers, and it includes the Nuratau Mountains, which are part of the western Tien Shan range, and the Kyzylkum Desert, which is one of the largest deserts in Central Asia. The biosphere reserve is home to more than 1,000 species of plants and animals, some of which are rare and endangered, such as the Ustyurt mountain sheep and the saiga antelope .

Hiking in the biosphere reserve allows you to explore the different landscapes, from the green and lush valleys and forests of the mountains, to the dry and barren plains and dunes of the desert. You can also admire the scenic views of the snow-capped peaks, the turquoise lakes, and the colorful rock formations. Along the way, you can encounter various wildlife, such as birds, reptiles, insects, and mammals.

Hiking in the biosphere reserve also allows you to learn about the rich and ancient culture and history of the local people, who belong to different ethnic groups, such as Tajiks, Uzbeks, Kazakhs, and Karakalpaks. You can visit some of the historical and religious sites that date back to thousands of years ago, such as Alexander's Fort, which was built by Alexander the Great in the 4th century BC, Chashma Spring, which is a sacred place for Muslims and Zoroastrians, and Beket Ata underground mosque, which is a pilgrimage site for Sufis. You can also stay in traditional yurts or guesthouses in rural villages, where you can experience the hospitality and lifestyle of the locals. You can taste their delicious cuisine, listen to their folk music, watch their dances, and join their festivals.

Hiking in the biosphere reserve is a rewarding and memorable adventure that will give you a glimpse of the beauty and diversity of Uzbekistan.

Camp at Aydarkul Lake

Camping at Aydarkul Lake is a wonderful way to experience the nature and culture of Uzbekistan. Aydarkul Lake is a large artificial lake that was formed as a result of a dam construction on the Syr Darya River in the 1960s. The lake covers an area of about 4,000 square kilometers, and it is surrounded by the Kyzylkum Desert and the Nuratau Mountains .

Camping at Aydarkul Lake offers you a chance to enjoy the tranquility and beauty of nature, as well as the fun and adventure of various activities. You can swim in the clear and refreshing water of the lake, which has a temperature of about 25°C in summer. You can also fish for carp, pike, perch, or catfish, which are abundant in the lake. You can also boat or kayak on the lake, and admire the views of the desert and the mountains. You can also birdwatch, as the lake attracts many migratory birds, such as pelicans, flamingos, ducks, geese, and cranes. You can also camel ride on the sandy shores of the lake, and experience the nomadic lifestyle of the local people.

Camping at Aydarkul Lake also has many benefits, such as experiencing the nomadic lifestyle, meeting friendly locals, or watching the stars at night. You can stay in traditional yurts, which are round tents made of felt and wood, and decorated with colorful patterns. You can also taste the delicious cuisine of the locals, such as pilaf, shashlik, or samsa. You can also listen to their folk music, watch their dances, and join their festivals. You can also watch the stars at night, as the sky is clear and dark, and you can see many constellations and planets.

Camping at Aydarkul Lake is a memorable and rewarding adventure that will make you appreciate the beauty and diversity of Uzbekistan.

Off-Roading in the Ustyurt Plateau

Embarking on an off-roading adventure in the Ustyurt Plateau unveils an expedition that will lead you to the most extraordinary and enigmatic landscapes in Central Asia. The Ustyurt Plateau, spanning across parts of Kazakhstan and Uzbekistan, offers a truly unique and diverse terrain, encompassing deserts, steppes, and towering cliffs. This remote region is also steeped in historical and cultural significance, having once been inhabited by ancient civilizations and nomadic tribes.

Off-roading in the Ustyurt Plateau is an opportunity to unveil the hidden treasures of this area. Discover ancient fortresses, underground mosques, salt marshes, chalk cliffs, and ingenious hunting traps. Explore the remnants of the Beleuli caravanserai, a 13th-century fortress that served as a Silk Road stopover for traders and travelers. Delve into the mystique of the Beket Ata underground mosque, carved into the rock by a renowned mystic, and cherished by Sufis. Marvel at the surreal Tuzbair salt marsh, a glistening salt flat mirroring the sky and the surrounding rock formations. Admire the striking Boszhyra natural boundary, a picturesque plateau adorned with white rock pillars resembling fangs. Encounter the remnants of ancient desert kites, cunningly devised for capturing saiga antelopes and other creatures.

Off-roading in the Ustyurt Plateau isn't for the faint of heart, as it demands resilience and adeptness. Harsh weather conditions, unforgiving terrain, and limited facilities will test your mettle. Navigate unpaved roads, sand dunes, gravel pits, and rocky slopes. Tolerate extreme temperatures, fierce winds, dust storms, and sandstorms. Come well-prepared with provisions, water, fuel, and equipment, as there are no road signs or maps to guide you. Be ready for any unforeseen emergencies or vehicle breakdowns.

The adventure of off-roading in the Ustyurt Plateau is a gratifying and unforgettable experience that will foster a deep appreciation for the sheer beauty and diversity of Central Asia.

Chapter 10. Culinary Secrets

Unique Regional Dishes

Uzbekistan is a country with a rich and diverse culinary heritage, influenced by its location along the ancient Silk Road, its nomadic and sedentary cultures, and its interactions with neighboring countries. Some of the dishes that are specific to a certain region or culture in Uzbekistan, and what makes them unique, are:

1. Plov is the national dish of Uzbekistan, and is prepared differently in each region. Plov is a rice dish cooked with meat, carrots, onions, spices, and sometimes dried fruits or nuts. Plov is usually cooked in a large cast-iron pot called a kazan over an open fire. Plov is often served on special occasions, such as weddings, birthdays, or holidays. Plov is also considered a symbol of hospitality and generosity.

2. Samsa is a baked or fried pastry filled with minced meat, onions, cheese, pumpkin, or potatoes. Samsa is shaped like a triangle or a half-moon, and is usually made with flaky dough or puff pastry. Samsa is often sold by street

vendors or in tea houses, and is a popular snack or appetizer. Samsa can be found in different regions of Uzbekistan, but the most famous ones are from the city of Bukhara.

3.   Shurpa is a hearty soup made with meat, vegetables, herbs, and spices. Shurpa can be cooked with lamb, beef, chicken, or fish, and can include potatoes, carrots, tomatoes, peppers, turnips, or beans. Shurpa is usually seasoned with cumin, coriander, turmeric, paprika, or saffron. Shurpa is a common dish in rural areas of Uzbekistan, where it is cooked in a clay pot over a wood fire.

4.   Manti are steamed dumplings filled with meat, onions, pumpkin, or spinach. Manti are usually made with thin dough and are shaped like small pouches. Manti are served with sour cream, butter, vinegar, or tomato sauce. Manti are a traditional dish in the Ferghana Valley of Uzbekistan, where they are often eaten for breakfast or lunch.

5.   Halva is a sweet confection made with sesame seeds, sugar, honey, nuts, or flour. Halva can be

soft or hard, and can have different flavors and colors. Halva is often eaten as a dessert or a treat during religious festivals or celebrations. Halva is a specialty of the city of Samarkand.

Hidden Food Markets

Uzbekistan boasts a diverse and culturally rich culinary heritage, deeply influenced by its strategic position along the ancient Silk Road, the interplay of nomadic and sedentary cultures, and interactions with neighboring nations. Amid this culinary tapestry, there exist some lesser-known and somewhat elusive food markets that serve as troves of authentic Uzbek flavors:

1. Chorsu Bazaar stands as Tashkent's oldest and largest market, located within the historical precincts near the Kukeldash Madrasah and the Juma Mosque. Navigating Chorsu Bazaar feels like wandering through a labyrinth of domed structures, teeming stalls, and vibrant crowds. It's a marketplace brimming with a wide array of fresh produce, aromatic spices, nuts, succulent meats, dairy products, freshly baked bread, and delectable sweets. Adventurous food enthusiasts can savor local delicacies like samsa, manti, shashlik, and plov. This bustling hub opens its doors from dawn till dusk.

1. Osh Bazaar, nestled in Osh, Uzbekistan's second-largest city and one of Central Asia's most ancient settlements, borders the Ak-Bura River, near the majestic Sulaiman-Too mountain. Osh Bazaar is renowned for its offering of dried fruits, nuts, and a treasure trove of spices, notably cumin cultivated in the nearby Fergana Valley. Beyond the culinary treasures, the market is celebrated for its crafts, including intricately woven carpets, pottery, artisan knives, and musical instruments. Osh Bazaar welcomes visitors daily from 8 am to 6 pm.

2. Khiva Bazaar adds an enchanting culinary and historical dimension within the UNESCO World Heritage Site of Khiva, one of Uzbekistan's most meticulously preserved cities. Located within the Ichan-Kala fortress, dating back to the 10th century, Khiva Bazaar transports visitors to the ambience of the ancient Silk Road, with its narrow alleyways, mud-brick homes, and resplendent mosques and minarets. Traditional Uzbek products, such as silk fabrics, carpets, jewelry, hats, and intricately crafted dolls, await those who explore its offerings. Khiva Bazaar welcomes guests daily from 9 am to 5 pm.

Chapter 11. Immersive Experiences

Staying with Locals

Staying with locals is one of the best ways to experience the authentic and diverse culture of Uzbekistan, as well as to make new friends and learn more about the country. However, staying with locals also comes with some challenges and responsibilities, as you need to respect and adapt to the cultural norms and expectations of both hosts and guests. Here are some tips on how to find and arrange such accommodation, and how to communicate and interact with locals.

1. To find and arrange local accommodation in Uzbekistan, you can use online platforms such as Airbnb, Couchsurfing, or Homestay.com, which connect travelers with local hosts who offer rooms or beds in their homes. You can also use travel agencies or tour operators that specialize in cultural tourism, such as Advantour, Kalpak Travel, or Silk Road Explore, which can arrange homestays, guesthouses, or yurts for you.

Alternatively, you can ask around in local cafes, shops, or mosques, or look for signs that say "mehmonkhona" (guesthouse) or "yurt" (traditional nomadic tent).

2. To communicate and interact with locals, you need to be aware of some basic etiquette and customs that are common in Uzbekistan. For example, you should always greet your hosts and guests with a handshake and a smile, and say "Assalomu alaykum" (peace be upon you) or "Salom" (hello). You should also remove your shoes before entering a house or a yurt, and dress modestly and respectfully. You should always accept any food or drink that is offered to you, and compliment your hosts on their hospitality and cooking. You should avoid topics such as politics, religion, or personal matters, unless your hosts initiate them. You should also respect the privacy and personal space of your hosts and guests, and ask for permission before taking photos or videos of them or their homes.

Some examples of the types of local accommodation available in Uzbekistan are:

- Homestays are where you stay with a local family in their home, usually in a rural area or a small town. Homestays are a great way to experience the daily life and culture of Uzbek people, as well as to enjoy their delicious home-cooked meals. Homestays are usually simple and comfortable, but may not have all the amenities that you are used to, such as hot water, internet, or air conditioning. Homestays are also a great opportunity to practice your Uzbek or Russian language skills, as most hosts do not speak English.

- Guesthouses are where you stay in a separate room or building within a local family's property, usually in a city or a tourist destination. Guesthouses are similar to homestays, but offer more privacy and independence. Guesthouses are usually clean and cozy, but may vary in quality and price depending on the location and the facilities. Guesthouses may also offer services such as laundry, breakfast, or transportation.

- Yurts are where you stay in a traditional nomadic tent made of felt and wood, usually in a desert or a mountain area. Yurts are a unique way to experience the nomadic heritage and lifestyle of Uzbek people, as well as to enjoy the natural beauty and scenery of Uzbekistan. Yurts are usually spacious and warm, but may not have any electricity or plumbing. Yurts are also a great opportunity to learn about the history and culture of Uzbek nomads, as well as to participate in activities such as camel riding, horse riding, or hiking.

Staying with locals is an immersive experience that can enrich your travel in Uzbekistan. However, you need to be respectful and adaptable to the cultural norms and expectations of both hosts and guests. By following these tips, you can find and arrange local accommodation that suits your needs and preferences, and communicate and interact with locals in a friendly and polite manner.

Participating in Local Festivities

Uzbekistan, with its rich and diverse cultural heritage, draws inspiration from its unique position along the ancient Silk Road, the fusion of nomadic and sedentary traditions, and its historical exchanges with neighboring lands. Throughout the year, the nation comes alive with various festivals and celebrations, inviting visitors to partake in the rich tapestry of Uzbek culture, traditions, and cuisine. Here, we explore some of the most vibrant and renowned festivals in Uzbekistan, and how you can immerse yourself in their festivities:

1. Navruz, a celebration marking the Persian New Year and the spring equinox, is an occasion of great significance in Uzbekistan, observed every March 21st. This national holiday epitomizes joy and festivity, symbolizing the rejuvenation of nature and life. Navruz comes to life with cultural performances, engaging games, and the preparation of a special dish known as sumalak, crafted from germinated wheat. The festival is also a time for reconnecting with friends and family, sharing gifts, and offering wishes of happiness and prosperity. To experience the vibrant spirit of Navruz in Uzbekistan, head to any city or town, where you'll encounter captivating concerts, bustling fairs, colorful parades, and dazzling fireworks. Don't forget to savor traditional Navruz dishes like samsa, pilaf, halva, and khalva.

2. Ramazan, the ninth month of the Islamic lunar calendar, signifies a sacred and spiritual period for Muslims in Uzbekistan. During this month, Muslims observe fasting, abstaining from food, drink, smoking, and worldly pleasures from dawn to dusk. Ramazan is also a time for prayer, Quran recitation, charitable acts, and aiding the less

fortunate. The conclusion of Ramazan is marked by Eid al-Fitr, the festive festival of breaking the fast. Eid al-Fitr is celebrated with prayers, feasts, the exchange of gifts, and visits to friends and family. To participate in and enjoy Ramazan in Uzbekistan, observe the fasting rules and refrain from eating or drinking in public during the daylight hours. You can also seize the opportunity to visit some of Uzbekistan's prominent mosques and madrasas, such as the grand Bibi-Khanym Mosque in Samarkand or the historic Kalyan Mosque in Bukhara. These sacred sites offer an authentic glimpse into the rituals and prayers associated with Ramazan. Additionally, consider joining some of the iftar meals provided by local restaurants or welcoming families after sunset.

3. Independence Day, celebrated on September 1, marks the national day of Uzbekistan, commemorating the nation's independence from the Soviet Union in 1991. Independence Day is a time of patriotism and festivity, when people express their pride and love for their country. The celebration includes official ceremonies, inspirational speeches, prestigious awards, and striking military parades. Cultural events, such as

concerts, dances, exhibitions, and spirited sports competitions, further enhance the festive spirit. To partake in and savor the atmosphere of Independence Day in Uzbekistan, head to the capital city of Tashkent, where the main festivities unfold at Independence Square. You can also enjoy captivating performances at the Alisher Navoi Opera and Ballet Theatre or be entertained by the marvels of the Tashkent Circus.

4. Silk and Spices Festival is an annual celebration that magnificently showcases the rich cultural and historical heritage of Bukhara, one of Uzbekistan's oldest cities and a former epicenter of trade and culture along the Silk Road. Typically held in June within various corners of Bukhara's historic old town, the Silk and Spices Festival presents bustling bazaars and fairs where you can acquire unique souvenirs and admire the craftsmanship of silk weavers, carpet artisans, potters, embroiderers, jewelry makers, and more. The festival comes alive with riveting live performances by musicians, dancers, and acrobats from across the nation and beyond, conjuring an atmosphere of ancient charm and beauty in Bukhara. To immerse yourself in the

magic of the Silk and Spices Festival in Uzbekistan, consider booking your tickets through reputable sources online, travel agencies, or tour operators specializing in cultural tourism. You can also participate in engaging workshops and contests organized during the festival.

These festivals provide an opportunity for visitors to become a part of Uzbekistan's cultural tapestry, offering a glimpse into the traditions, celebrations, and flavors that define this enchanting nation. Join in the festivities and create lasting memories while experiencing the very best of Uzbek culture.

Chapter 12. Language and Communication

Local Dialects

The Uzbek language is a Turkic language that belongs to the Karluk branch, along with Uyghur and Chagatai. The Uzbek language has many dialects that are spoken in various regions of Uzbekistan, and they differ from the standard Uzbek language in terms of vocabulary, pronunciation, or grammar. The dialects of Uzbek are influenced by the historical and geographical factors that shaped the development of the Uzbek people and their culture. The dialects of Uzbek also affect the communication and identity of the speakers, as they reflect their regional and ethnic diversity.

Some of the main dialects of Uzbek are:

1. Oghuz is a dialect that is spoken in the Khorezm region of Uzbekistan, as well as in Turkmenistan and Iran. Oghuz is derived from the Oghuz Turks, who migrated to Central Asia from the 10th century onwards. Oghuz is characterized by its use of the /g/ sound instead of the /k/ sound in

some words, such as "gul" (flower) instead of "kul" (standard Uzbek), or "goy" (blue) instead of "koy" (standard Uzbek). Oghuz also has some words that are different from standard Uzbek, such as "yashil" (green) instead of "sabz" (standard Uzbek), or "yol" (road) instead of "yo'l" (standard Uzbek).

2. Kipchak is a dialect that is spoken in the Tashkent region of Uzbekistan, as well as in Kazakhstan and Kyrgyzstan. Kipchak is derived from the Kipchak Turks, who dominated Central Asia from the 11th to the 13th centuries. Kipchak is characterized by its use of the /sh/ sound instead of the /s/ sound in some words, such as "shirin" (sweet) instead of "sirin" (standard Uzbek), or "shahar" (city) instead of "sahar" (standard Uzbek). Kipchak also has some words that are different from standard Uzbek, such as "kazan" (pot) instead of "qozon" (standard Uzbek), or "kara" (black) instead of "qora" (standard Uzbek).

3. Karluk is a dialect that is spoken in the Fergana Valley region of Uzbekistan, as well as in Tajikistan and Afghanistan. Karluk is derived from the Karluk Turks, who settled in Central

Asia from the 9th century onwards. Karluk is characterized by its use of the /ch/ sound instead of the /j/ sound in some words, such as "chayon" (tea) instead of "jayon" (standard Uzbek), or "chiziq" (line) instead of "jiziq" (standard Uzbek). Karluk also has some words that are different from standard Uzbek, such as "tovush" (sound) instead of "tovus" (standard Uzbek), or "toshbaqa" (turtle) instead of "toshbaqa" (standard Uzbek).

4. Sart is a dialect that is spoken in the Samarkand and Bukhara regions of Uzbekistan, as well as in Turkmenistan and Afghanistan. Sart is derived from the Sarts, who were a mixed group of Turkic and Iranian peoples who lived in Central Asia from the 13th to the 19th centuries. Sart is characterized by its use of the /z/ sound instead of the /j/ sound in some words, such as "zamon" (time) instead of "jamon" (standard Uzbek), or "zavod" (factory) instead of "javod" (standard Uzbek). Sart also has some words that are different from standard Uzbek, such as "pulat" (steel) instead of "polad" (standard Uzbek), or "bazar" (market) instead of "bozor" (standard Uzbek).

These dialects of Uzbek are not mutually intelligible with each other or with standard Uzbek, which is based on the Tashkent dialect. Therefore, speakers of different dialects may need to use standard Uzbek or Russian to communicate with each other. However, these dialects also represent the rich and diverse heritage and identity of the Uzbek people, and are an important part of their culture.

Learning Basic Phrases

Learning some basic phrases in Uzbek or Russian, which are the most widely spoken languages in Uzbekistan, can have many benefits and challenges for travelers. Learning some basic phrases can help you communicate better with locals, appreciate their culture more, and have a more enjoyable travel experience. However, learning some basic phrases can also be difficult and frustrating, as you may encounter different dialects, accents, or scripts that are hard to understand or pronounce. Here are some examples of the most useful and common phrases in Uzbek or Russian, and how to pronounce them correctly.

Greetings: Greeting someone is a polite and friendly way to start a conversation or show respect. Some of the most common greetings in Uzbek or Russian are:

- Assalomu alaykum (Peace be upon you) or Salom (Hello) in Uzbek. These are used to greet anyone at any time of the day. You can respond with Va alaykum assalom (And peace be upon you) or Salom (Hello). To pronounce them, say "ah-sah-loh-moo ah-lay-koom" or "sah-lohm" in Uzbek.

- Zdravstvuyte (Hello) or Privet (Hi) in Russian. These are used to greet anyone at any time of the day. You can respond with the same words. To pronounce them, say "zdrah-stvooy-tyeh" or "pree-vyet" in Russian.

Introductions: Introducing yourself or someone else is a way to share some basic information or establish a connection. Some of the most common phrases for introductions in Uzbek or Russian are:

- Mening ismim ... (My name is ...) or Men ... danman (I am from ...) in Uzbek. These are used to tell someone your name or where you are from. You can ask someone else's name or origin by saying Sizning ismingiz nima? (What is your name?) or Siz qayerdan? (Where are you from?). To pronounce them, say "meh-nin ees-meem ..." or "mehn ... dahn-mahn" in Uzbek.

- Menya zovut ... (My name is ...) or Ya iz ... (I am from ...) in Russian. These are used to tell someone your name or where you are from. You can ask someone else's name or origin by saying Kak vas zovut? (What is your name?) or Otkuda vy? (Where are you from?). To pronounce them, say "meh-nya zoh-voot ..." or "yah eez ..." in Russian.

Requests: Making a request is a way to ask for something that you need or want. Some of the most common phrases for requests in Uzbek or Russian are:

- Iltimos ... (Please ...) or Rahmat ... (Thank you ...) in Uzbek. These are used to make a polite request or express gratitude for something. You can also say Kechirasiz ... (Excuse me ...) to get someone's attention or apologize for something. To pronounce them, say "eel-tee-mohs ..." or "rah-hmaht ..." in Uzbek.

- Pozhaluysta ... (Please ...) or Spasibo ... (Thank you ...) in Russian. These are used to make a polite request or express gratitude for something. You can also say Izvinite ... (Excuse me ...) to get someone's attention or apologize for something.

To pronounce them, say "pah-zhah-loo-stah ..." or "spah-see-bah ..." in Russian.

Expressions of gratitude: Expressing gratitude is a way to show appreciation or kindness for something that someone has done for you. Some of the most common expressions of gratitude in Uzbek or Russian are:

- Rahmat (Thank you) or Katta rahmat (Thank you very much) in Uzbek. These are used to thank someone for anything that they have done for you. You can also say Juda rahmat (Thanks a lot) to emphasize your gratitude. To pronounce them, say "rah-hmaht" or "kah-ttah rah-hmaht" in Uzbek.
- Spasibo (Thank you) or Bolshoye spasibo (Thank you very much) in Russian. These are used to thank someone for anything that they have done for you. You can also say Ogromnoye spasibo (Thanks a lot) to emphasize your gratitude. To pronounce them, say "spah-see-bah" or "bahl-shoh-yeh spah-see-bah" in Russian.

These are some of the most useful and common phrases in Uzbek or Russian that can help you communicate better with locals, appreciate their culture more, and have a more enjoyable travel experience. However, you should also be aware that these phrases may vary depending on the dialect, accent, or script that the speaker uses. Therefore, you should also try to listen carefully, speak slowly, and use gestures or pictures to help you understand and be understood. Learning some basic phrases in Uzbek or Russian can be challenging, but also rewarding and fun.

Chapter 12. Traveling Responsibly

Sustainable Tourism Practices

Sustainable tourism in Uzbekistan is a responsible and mindful approach to travel that prioritizes the conservation of the country's natural and cultural heritage while fostering its social and economic development. This commitment to sustainability is of paramount importance in Uzbekistan as it strives to preserve its diverse landscapes, historical treasures, and cultural traditions. Simultaneously, it seeks to enhance the well-being and quality of life for its inhabitants. However, Uzbekistan faces a series of challenges that pose threats to its natural and cultural resources, including issues such as water scarcity, pollution, deforestation, and urbanization.

Here are some of the key issues and threats impacting Uzbekistan's natural and cultural heritage:

1. Water Scarcity: Uzbekistan is among the world's most arid countries, with a meager average annual rainfall of 200 mm. Water is a

fundamental resource for agriculture, industry, and daily life, but it remains scarce and unequally distributed. The nation is heavily reliant on water from the Amu Darya and Syr Darya rivers, originating in neighboring Tajikistan and Kyrgyzstan. These rivers are subject to climate change, overuse, and pollution, which result in diminished flow and quality. Water scarcity presents a significant obstacle to sustainable tourism by limiting water availability for both tourists and local residents.

2. Pollution: Uzbekistan contends with various forms of pollution that adversely affect its environment and public health. Air pollution is a consequence of emissions from vehicles, factories, power plants, and the incineration of waste. Water pollution arises from untreated sewage, industrial waste, agricultural runoff, and mining operations. Soil pollution is driven by the use of pesticides, fertilizers, and salinization. Pollution negatively impacts Uzbekistan's natural beauty, biodiversity, and the well-being of its people. Furthermore, it diminishes the appeal and safety of sustainable tourism by detracting from the allure and comfort of visiting natural and cultural sites.

3. Deforestation: Uzbekistan has a limited forest cover, primarily concentrated in mountainous regions, accounting for only 7.6% of its territory. Forests are vital for ecological balance, biodiversity, and provide various benefits such as timber, fuelwood, food, medicine, and recreational spaces. Deforestation is exacerbated by logging, mining, agriculture, urbanization, and wildfires. It leads to soil erosion, desertification, habitat loss, reduced biodiversity, and climate change. Deforestation undermines the potential and viability of sustainable tourism in Uzbekistan as it eradicates the natural resources and landscapes that attract tourists.

4. Urbanization: Uzbekistan is undergoing rapid urbanization, with over half of its population residing in urban areas. Urbanization is driven by economic development, social mobility, and population growth. It offers both positive and negative consequences for sustainable tourism. While it creates more infrastructure, services, and opportunities for tourists and locals, it can also result in congestion, noise, waste, crime, and the erosion of cultural identity. Urbanization can also

give rise to conflicts between urban and rural areas over resource distribution and utilization.

These are the principal challenges and opportunities associated with practicing sustainable tourism in Uzbekistan. Travelers can adopt a series of sustainable tourism practices to minimize their environmental and social footprint while exploring the country:

1. Utilize Public Transportation or Bicycles: Choose public transportation or bicycles over private cars or taxis to reduce your carbon footprint, save money, and immerse yourself in the local culture.

2. Select Eco-Friendly Accommodations: Opt for eco-friendly accommodations such as homestays, guesthouses, or yurts, which utilize renewable energy sources, recycle materials, and employ local staff. This helps conserve water and energy resources, reduce waste, and support local communities.

3. Support Local Businesses: Contribute to local economic development by patronizing local businesses or communities instead of

multinational corporations or chains. Buy souvenirs from local artisans, dine at local restaurants, or engage in local tours and activities.

4. Volunteer for Conservation or Social Projects: Enhance your travel experience by volunteering for projects related to wildlife conservation, environmental education, cultural preservation, or community service. Your efforts can contribute to the protection and restoration of Uzbekistan's natural and cultural heritage, as well as its social and economic advancement.

These practices not only enrich your travel experience in Uzbekistan but also make a positive impact on the environment and its people. By adopting sustainable tourism principles, you can play a role in preserving the country's remarkable natural and cultural resources for future generations.

Chapter 13. Safety and Health in Less Touristy Areas

Travel Precautions

Traveling in less touristy areas in Uzbekistan can be an adventurous and rewarding experience, as you can explore the hidden gems and authentic aspects of the country. However, traveling in less touristy areas also comes with some potential risks and dangers, such as political instability, crime, scams, or health issues. Therefore, it is important to take some travel precautions to avoid or cope with these risks and dangers, and to ensure a safe and enjoyable travel experience.

Some of the travel precautions that you should take are:

1. Planning ahead: Before you travel to less touristy areas in Uzbekistan, you should plan ahead and research the destination. You should check the latest travel advice and warnings from your government or embassy, and register your travel plans with them. You should also book your accommodation and transportation in advance,

and have a backup plan in case of emergency. You should also prepare a travel kit that includes your passport, visa, insurance, money, medication, and emergency contacts.

2. Following the local laws and customs: When you travel to less touristy areas in Uzbekistan, you should respect and follow the local laws and customs. You should avoid any political or religious demonstrations or discussions, as they may be sensitive or illegal. You should also dress modestly and conservatively, especially when visiting mosques or madrasas. You should also avoid drinking alcohol or smoking in public places, as they may be frowned upon or prohibited.

3. Avoiding border regions: When you travel to less touristy areas in Uzbekistan, you should avoid the border regions with neighboring countries, such as Afghanistan, Tajikistan, Kyrgyzstan, Kazakhstan, or Turkmenistan. These border regions may be unstable, unsafe, or restricted. You may encounter landmines, armed groups, smugglers, or border guards. You may also need special permits or visas to enter these border regions.

4. Being alert to scams or crime: When you travel to less touristy areas in Uzbekistan, you should be alert to scams or crime that may target tourists. You should beware of pickpockets, robbers, or fraudsters who may try to steal your money or belongings. You should also avoid exchanging money on the black market, as you may get counterfeit or invalid currency. You should also be careful of taxi drivers who may overcharge you or take you to the wrong destination.

These are some of the travel precautions that you should take when traveling in less touristy areas in Uzbekistan. By following these precautions, you can minimize your risks and dangers, and maximize your safety and enjoyment.

Health Facilities and Services

Safety and Health in Less Touristy Areas in Uzbekistan

This book aims to provide valuable tips and information to help travelers stay safe and healthy while exploring Uzbekistan's less touristy regions.

Health Facilities and Services:

Access to quality healthcare is a crucial consideration for travelers, particularly in less touristy areas of Uzbekistan. The quality and availability of healthcare facilities and services can vary depending on the location and the type of care needed.

Uzbekistan operates a public healthcare system funded by the government and mandatory health insurance, which offers a basic package of services to all citizens. However, it's essential to note that many health services, including primary, secondary, and tertiary care, may fall outside this package and require out-of-pocket payments or private health insurance.

In urban areas, private healthcare facilities are more readily available and provide a higher quality of care but at a higher cost. Before traveling, it's advisable to check your travel insurance coverage to ensure it caters to your health needs. Travelers should be prepared to cover any medical services not covered by insurance or the public healthcare system and keep receipts for potential reimbursement or tax purposes.

Some of the healthcare facilities and services you can expect in less touristy areas of Uzbekistan are:

1. Hospitals: These facilities are the primary providers of secondary and tertiary care. They offer services such as surgery, intensive care, radiology, laboratory work, pharmacy services, and rehabilitation. Hospitals are commonly located in regional or district centers and may be either public or private. While public hospitals tend to be more cost-effective, they may have longer waiting times, limited resources, or lower quality. In contrast, private hospitals offer quicker services, higher quality care, and more resources but at a higher cost.

2. Clinics: Clinics are the main providers of primary care. They offer services like general medicine, pediatrics, gynecology, cardiology, and dentistry. Clinics are typically situated in both rural and urban areas, and like hospitals, they can be either public or private. Public clinics are more budget-friendly but may have longer waiting times, fewer resources, or lower quality care. On the other hand, private clinics offer quicker service, higher quality, and better resources, but at a higher cost.

3. Pharmacies: Pharmacies are where you can purchase medicines and medical supplies in Uzbekistan. They offer a wide range of products, including prescription drugs, over-the-counter medications, vitamins, and hygiene items. Pharmacies are commonly found in both rural and urban areas and may be either public or private. Public pharmacies are often more affordable but may have limited stock and availability. Private pharmacies, though pricier, generally have more stock and better availability. It's vital to check the expiration date and quality of the medicines before making a purchase.

4. Ambulance Services: Ambulance services are responsible for providing emergency care and transportation. They offer services like first aid, resuscitation, and referrals. Ambulance services are typically available in both rural and urban areas and are free of charge for all citizens and residents. You can request an ambulance service by calling 103. However, it's worth noting that ambulance response times and quality may vary based on the location and the situation.

Specific Health Concerns for Travelers in Uzbekistan:

Travelers in Uzbekistan need to be aware of specific health concerns that they should take precautions against. Some of these include:

- COVID-19: The ongoing COVID-19 pandemic poses a global health concern. Travelers are advised to stay updated with their government's or embassy's travel advice and restrictions regarding COVID-19. Travelers should also adhere to the health and safety measures implemented by Uzbek authorities, including mask-wearing, social distancing, frequent hand washing, and vaccination.

- Vaccinations: Ensuring that you are up-to-date with routine vaccinations, such as MMR (measles-mumps-rubella),DTP(diphtheria-tetanus -pertussis), polio, hepatitis A and B, and influenza is essential. Additionally, travelers should consider additional vaccinations that may be recommended or required for Uzbekistan, such as typhoid, rabies, meningitis, yellow fever, or cholera. It's advisable to consult with your doctor or a travel clinic at least 4 to 6 weeks before your trip to receive the necessary vaccinations and advice.

- Food and Water Safety: Travelers should be cautious about their food and water choices in Uzbekistan to avoid exposure to foodborne or waterborne diseases like diarrhea, dysentery, hepatitis A or E, typhoid fever, or cholera. Precautions include avoiding raw or undercooked meat, seafood, eggs, and dairy products, as well as unwashed or unpeeled fruits and vegetables. Drinking only bottled or boiled water is essential, while avoiding ice cubes, tap water, and unpasteurized drinks is advisable.

- Tick-Borne Diseases: In rural areas of Uzbekistan, especially during the warmer months, tick-borne diseases transmitted by ticks pose a significant risk. Such diseases can lead to symptoms like fever, headache, rash, and joint pain, with potential complications including meningitis, encephalitis, or hemorrhagic fever. Various tick-borne diseases exist, such as Lyme disease, Crimean-Congo hemorrhagic fever, Q fever, and tick-borne encephalitis. To mitigate these risks, travelers should avoid walking in tall grass or wooded areas, wear long-sleeved clothing and pants, use insect repellent, and conduct tick checks on themselves and pets after outdoor activities.

The Importance of Travel Insurance:

Travel insurance is a vital component of travel preparations, ensuring that you are financially protected against unexpected costs and losses while on your journey. Here's why travel insurance is indispensable:

1. Medical Expenses: Travel insurance covers the costs of medical treatment, hospitalization, medications, and evacuation in the event of illness or injury during travel. This is a crucial safeguard against high out-of-pocket expenses or the risk of being denied care in some regions.

2. Trip Cancellations or Interruptions: Travel plans can change due to unforeseen circumstances. Travel insurance provides financial protection if you must cancel or cut your trip short due to reasons like illness, injury, natural disasters, or civil unrest.

3. Baggage Loss or Delay: Losing or damaging personal belongings or baggage can be an inconvenience. Travel insurance can cover the costs of replacing or repairing lost, stolen, or damaged items, alleviating the financial burden.

4. Personal Liability: Travel insurance provides coverage for legal fees or compensation if you cause damage or injury to someone else's property or person during your travels. This protection can help you avoid potential lawsuits or claims.

5. Emergency Assistance: Travel insurance offers 24/7 emergency assistance and support to help resolve any issues or difficulties encountered during your journey. This can include providing information, advice, referrals, translation services, or coordination of services.

Travel insurance is especially vital for travelers venturing into less touristy areas of Uzbek

Chapter 14. Booking Accommodation in Hidden-Gem Locations

Guesthouses and Boutique Hotels

When it comes to finding suitable accommodation, particularly in less touristy areas, travelers may face challenges like limited options or high costs. In this article, we'll introduce you to guesthouses and boutique hotels, two types of lodging that offer unique and comfortable stays in Uzbekistan's hidden-gem locations.

Understanding Guesthouses and Boutique Hotels

Guesthouses and boutique hotels stand out among accommodation options due to their distinctive characteristics in terms of size, style, and service:

1. Guesthouses: These are cozy, intimate establishments that offer lodging and breakfast for travelers. Typically, guesthouses are managed by local families or individuals who either reside

on the premises or nearby. They create a welcoming and homely atmosphere where travelers can interact with hosts and fellow guests. Guesthouses may provide private or shared rooms and bathrooms, with pricing and availability being key determinants.

2. Boutique Hotels: These are small, stylish establishments that provide lodging and additional services to travelers. Boutique hotels are often designed around a theme or concept that reflects local culture or history. Expect personalized and attentive services with a variety of amenities and facilities. Boutique hotels typically offer different types of rooms and suites, catering to various price points and availability.

Travelers who venture into less touristy areas of Uzbekistan and opt for guesthouses and boutique hotels can experience a range of benefits and drawbacks:

Advantages:

- Cultural Immersion: Guesthouses and boutique hotels offer travelers a unique and authentic encounter with local culture and lifestyle. Interacting with hosts and staff provides insights into the region's history, traditions, and customs. It's an opportunity to savor local cuisine and engage in regional events and activities.

- Comfort in Less Touristy Areas: These establishments provide comfortable and convenient stays in less touristy regions. Travelers can relish the privacy, tranquility, and charm offered by guesthouses and boutique hotels, often situated close to main attractions. The personalized service adds to the allure.

- Value for Money: Travelers can find good value in guesthouses and boutique hotels in less touristy areas. These establishments often offer cost-effective options compared to other types of accommodation. While being budget-friendly, they don't skimp on features and services.

Disadvantages:

- Limited Availability: Guesthouses and boutique hotels may be less available and accessible in less touristy areas, especially during peak seasons or holidays. Finding and booking these accommodations might be challenging.

Additionally, transportation to and from remote or rural areas could pose difficulties.

- Varied Quality: Quality and consistency in guesthouses and boutique hotels can be somewhat unpredictable in less touristy areas. Travelers may encounter issues such as hygiene concerns, maintenance problems, security issues, or communication difficulties. Standards, policies, and expectations might differ among these establishments.

- Fewer Options: These accommodations may offer fewer choices in terms of room types, sizes, or views. Amenities and facilities may also be more limited compared to larger hotels. Features like internet access, air conditioning, or a swimming pool may be less common.

Examples of the Best Guesthouses and Boutique Hotels in Uzbekistan

1. Mirzo Boutique Hotel: Situated in Tashkent, Mirzo Boutique Hotel opened its doors in 2019. The establishment boasts a garden, terrace, restaurant, bar, and a range of amenities such as

24-hour front desk, airport transfers, and free WiFi. The rooms are well-appointed with modern amenities. Guests can enjoy city views from some rooms. The hotel also offers bike and car rentals, making it easy for travelers to explore. You can find Mirzo Boutique Hotel on popular booking platforms such as Booking.com or its official website.

2. Kukaldosh Boutique Hotel: This minimalist boutique hotel located in Bukhara opened in 2018. Its central location near the Lyabi-Hauz in the old town makes it a convenient choice for travelers. The rooms are spacious and comfortable, and the staff is known for their friendliness and helpfulness. Kukaldosh Boutique Hotel is listed on platforms like Tripadvisor and has its official website for reservations.

3. Hotel Uzbekistan: With a history dating back to 1974, Hotel Uzbekistan in Tashkent provides a family-friendly atmosphere and a range of amenities, including air conditioning, a minibar, and seating areas. It also offers free internet access. The hotel features a 24-hour front desk, a concierge, and room service for guests' convenience. If you're driving, free parking is

available. The hotel's proximity to various attractions makes it an excellent choice for exploring Tashkent.

For travelers seeking to explore hidden-gem locations in Uzbekistan, guesthouses and boutique hotels offer distinctive and memorable lodging options. It's essential for travelers to weigh the advantages and disadvantages before choosing such accommodations. Fortunately, guesthouses and boutique hotels can be found in various regions and cities in Uzbekistan. Travelers can make use of online platforms and websites to discover, book, and enjoy the authentic and diverse aspects of Uzbekistan during their stay.

Online Booking Tips

Online Booking Tips for Accommodation in Hidden-Gem Locations in Uzbekistan

Uzbekistan, with its abundant cultural and natural heritage, beckons travelers to explore its wonders. From the ancient cities of Samarkand, Bukhara, and Khiva to the breathtaking landscapes of the Aral Sea, the Kyzylkum Desert, and the Pamir Mountains, Uzbekistan caters to every kind of traveler. Yet, securing suitable accommodation in this country can be challenging, especially in less touristy areas where options might be limited or expensive. In this article, we will provide valuable tips and tricks for booking accommodation online in Uzbekistan's hidden-gem locations.

The Advantages of Booking Online

Choosing to book accommodation online when planning your trip to Uzbekistan offers numerous advantages, including:

- Time and Cost Savings: Online booking provides a convenient platform to compare prices, availability, and reviews of various accommodation options all in one place. You can save money and time by doing this. Additionally, online platforms and websites often offer discounts, deals, and rewards, helping you make the most of your budget while avoiding commissions or fees to travel agents.

- A Plethora of Choices and Flexibility: Online booking opens up a world of accommodation options in Uzbekistan, ranging from hotels, hostels, and apartments to guesthouses, yurts, and homestays. The vast selection allows you to tailor your stay according to your preferences. With search filters by location, price, rating, amenities, or style, you have the flexibility to meet your specific requirements. Furthermore, if your plans change, online booking allows you to modify or cancel your reservations with ease.

- Access to Detailed Information and Assurance: Online booking provides a wealth of information about your accommodation choices. You can read in-depth descriptions, view photos, and peruse guest reviews to ensure a clear understanding of your potential lodging. You can also communicate directly with hosts or staff through online platforms and websites, securing instant confirmation and receipts for your bookings.

The Challenges and Risks of Booking Online

While online booking comes with many benefits, it also carries its share of challenges and risks:

- Limited Availability and Accessibility: Some less touristy areas in Uzbekistan may have limited online availability, often due to unreliable or slow internet connections. Certain accommodation options may not be listed or regularly updated on online platforms. Communicating with hosts or staff may be difficult in these areas.

- Quality and Consistency Issues: In less touristy regions of Uzbekistan, you may encounter variations in quality and consistency among accommodation options. Some may not align with their descriptions, photos, or reviews, and hosts may not deliver promised services or facilities. In some cases, bookings could be canceled or changed without prior notice or compensation.

- Scams and Frauds: Travelers booking online should be cautious of potential scams and frauds that may target them. Untrustworthy online platforms or websites might deceive travelers. Additionally, some hosts or staff members may act unprofessionally, leading to overpriced or invalid bookings.

The Best Online Platforms and Websites for Booking Accommodation in Uzbekistan

Several online platforms and websites cater to travelers looking to book accommodation in Uzbekistan. Here are some noteworthy examples of platforms and effective strategies for their use:

- Booking.com: Booking.com ranks among the most popular and extensively used online platforms for accommodation bookings globally. It features a diverse array of lodging choices in Uzbekistan, including hotels, hostels, apartments, guesthouses, yurts, and homestays. With its user-friendly interface, you can seamlessly filter searches based on location, price, rating, amenities, or style. Booking.com is also known for its reliable customer service, offering 24/7 support, free cancellation options, and best price guarantees. To make the most of Booking.com, remember to book well in advance, read reviews thoroughly for accurate impressions, understand the cancellation policies, and utilize the direct contact feature for inquiries.

- Caravanistan: Caravanistan serves as a specialized online platform for booking accommodation in Central Asia. It curates an updated selection of lodging options in Uzbekistan, encompassing hotels, hostels,

133

apartments, guesthouses, yurts, and homestays. Caravanistan's comprehensive guide provides vital travel information and tips, covering areas like visas, registration, transportation, and local attractions. The platform's friendly community is also available to offer travelers advice and support. When using Caravanistan, focus your search on hidden-gem locations by region or city, pay close attention to detailed descriptions and reviews, directly verify availability and prices, and participate in the platform's forum and contact form for inquiries and feedback.

- KAYAK: KAYAK is a comprehensive online platform that facilitates bookings for accommodations, flights, car rentals, and more, all within one platform. KAYAK offers a diverse selection of accommodation options in Uzbekistan, encompassing hotels, hostels, apartments, guesthouses, yurts, and homestays. With its robust search engine, you can compare prices, availability, and reviews from various online platforms and websites. The platform's flexibility and convenience enable you to modify or cancel bookings effortlessly when plans change. To optimize your use of KAYAK, leverage its filters and tools to refine your search, use the map feature to assess accommodation proximity to main attractions, set price alerts for deals, and manage bookings via the app or website.

Booking accommodation online is a convenient, reliable, and cost-effective method for planning your trip to hidden-gem locations in Uzbekistan. This approach provides benefits such as time and cost savings, an extensive range of choices, and detailed information. However, travelers should remain vigilant regarding the challenges and risks of booking online, including limited availability, quality and consistency variations, and potential scams. By adhering to the tips and tricks provided here and utilizing trustworthy online platforms and websites like Booking.com, Caravanistan, and KAYAK, you can ensure a memorable and authentic Uzbekistan experience.

Chapter 16. Conclusion

Uzbekistan, a land brimming with rich cultural and natural heritage, invites travelers to embark on a remarkable journey. From the timeless cities of Samarkand, Bukhara, and Khiva, to the breathtaking landscapes of the Aral Sea, the Kyzylkum Desert, and the Pamir Mountains, Uzbekistan offers something to enthrall every visitor. Yet, beyond these famed attractions, Uzbekistan conceals numerous hidden gems, eagerly awaiting discovery by intrepid and inquisitive travelers. These hidden gems are the less-traveled, less touristy areas that promise a unique and authentic glimpse into the local culture and lifestyle.

In this book, we present you with valuable tips and essential information to aid in your exploration of Uzbekistan's hidden gems. We cover various topics, including:

1. Choosing the Ideal Time to Visit Uzbekistan:

To truly relish your Uzbekistan experience, it's essential to consider the best time and season for your visit. Uzbekistan's diverse landscapes and attractions may be better enjoyed during specific months or climatic conditions.

2. Navigating Visa and Registration Requirements:

Uzbekistan has specific visa and registration prerequisites that travelers need to be aware of before embarking on their journey. Understanding these requirements is crucial to ensure a hassle-free visit.

3. Prioritizing Safety and Health Precautions:

Safety and health should always be paramount during your travels. We provide you with insights into how to stay healthy and secure in Uzbekistan, whether you're exploring vibrant markets or remote desert regions.

4. Choosing the Right Accommodation Options:

Your choice of lodging is crucial in determining how you will experience your trip. We offer guidance on selecting the best places to stay, whether you prefer the comfort of hotels, the charm of guesthouses, or the authenticity of homestays.

5. Leveraging the Best Travel Resources:

Uzbekistan's hidden gems may not always be visible through traditional travel channels. We share insights into finding the most reliable resources for planning and executing your adventure.

I hope this book has kindled your curiosity and desire to explore Uzbekistan's less touristy areas. Moreover, I trust that the information provided will assist you in preparing, planning, and savoring every moment of your Uzbekistan journey. **Here are a few recommendations to make the most of your adventure:**

Cultivate Flexibility and Open-Mindedness:

Uzbekistan is a country known for its diversity and intricacy. Embrace unforeseen situations and relish new experiences. Demonstrate respect and a genuine curiosity for the local culture and the warm-hearted people you'll meet along your journey.

Embrace Adventure and Ingenuity:

Uzbekistan may challenge you with its remoteness and unique character. Be ready to venture outside your comfort zone and embrace the unfamiliar. Be imaginative and resourceful in the face of challenges, as this will enhance your travel experience.

Practice Gratitude and Generosity:

Uzbekistan's charm often lies in the beauty of its landscapes and the hospitality of its people. Remember to express gratitude for the kindness and generosity of your hosts and the local community. Be generous in sharing your experiences, and your feedback and appreciation can become a source of mutual enrichment.

Uzbekistan, with its hidden gems, is a destination that beckons travelers. Don't let this opportunity to explore a new and thrilling destination slip through your fingers. Book your journey to Uzbekistan today and set out to uncover its splendid hidden treasures!

Made in United States
Troutdale, OR
03/03/2024

18170161R00080